Slag & Marble Glass
THE PROMINENT YEARS, 1959-1985
Imperial, Westmoreland, L. G. Wright, and Fenton

NATHAN TAVES & DON JENNINGS

4880 Lower Valley Road   Atglen, Pennsylvania 19310

Dedication

To Irene Anna Mabel Tews who introduced us to the joy of collecting glass.

To Carl W. Gustkey and Lucile Kennedy who reintroduced the world to Slag Glass at the Imperial Glass Corporation.

Published by Schiffer Publishing Ltd.
4880 Lower Valley Road
Atglen, PA 19310
Phone: (610) 593-1777; Fax: (610) 593-2002
E-mail: Info@schifferbooks.com

Copyright © 2007 by Nathan Taves & Don Jennings
Library of Congress Control Number: 2007920916

Designed by "Sue"
Type set in Piranesl It BT/Zurich BT

ISBN: 978-0-7643-2652-3
Printed in China

For the largest selection of fine reference books on this and related subjects, please visit our web site at www. schifferbooks.com
We are always looking for people to write books on new and related subjects. If you have an idea for a book please contact us at the above address.

This book may be purchased from the publisher.
Include $3.95 for shipping.
Please try your bookstore first.
You may write for a free catalog.

In Europe, Schiffer books are distributed by
Bushwood Books
6 Marksbury Ave.
Kew Gardens
Surrey TW9 4JF England
Phone: 44 (0) 20 8392-8585; Fax: 44 (0) 20 8392-9876
E-mail: info@bushwoodbooks.co.uk
Website: www.bushwoodbooks.co.uk
Free postage in the U.K., Europe; air mail at cost.

Contents

Acknowledgments

Thank you: Edna Barnes, Judy Bennett, Sharon & Chuck Bragg, Joan Cimini, Tom Felt, Frank Fenton, Don Frazier, Myrna & Bob Garrison, Geraldine Gentry, Carol and Paul Hrics, Gary Kearney & Todd Barkes, Carolyn Kaiser Rapp, Lucile Kennedy for many reasons, Willard Kolb for his devotion to glass factory records, Lorraine Kovar, Buella Lawson, Gary & Dodie Levi for many reasons, Kent P. Longwell, Terry Marsh, Jim Measell who always had time for questions, Tim Mosser, Blanche & William Murner, Jerry Parsons, Lois Ratcliff, Wilma and Richard Ross, Flo Ross, Phil Rosso, Jr., Diane Romine & Leslie Gallo, W. C. "Red" Roetteis, O. J. Scherschligt, Leah and Jay Simmons, and Karen & Alan Wells.

We extend a very special thanks to Kay & Don Sidwell and Georgia & Roger Brown for loaning several items to be photographed and documented in this book.

We also extend a very special thanks to Laura Marsh and our sister-in-law, Christine Tews, for editorial advice. You both were a great help!

Thanks to everyone at Accu-Color Lab Inc. and Sunny Schick Camera Shop.

All photographs were taken by Nathan Taves using a Pentax K1000 35mm camera and Fujifilm Velvia 100F daylight film.

The authors can be contacted at:
nathantaves@aol.com
or P. O. Box #151, Churubusco, IN, 46723.

Note: No Slag Glass was harmed during the photographing and writing of this book.

Preface

Almost all glass collectors have stories of how they came to collecting. In general, I credit my mom, Irene Tews. I grew up with her glass collection. Her tastes were eclectic and the shelves of our home included Carnival Glass compotes, Milk Glass animal dishes, and bottles from Blenko Glass. My specific story dates back to 1976 when I bought a small Slag Glass dog made by the Degenhart Glass Company. Under the mastery of Bernard C. Boyd, Degenhart was making a wonderful assortment of Slag colors and I was soon hooked on collecting Slag. My fascination must have been infectious. Soon, my mom also started collecting Slag glass. We eventually learned of other factories that had been making Slag such as Imperial and Westmoreland. At the time, I was finishing college and with my limited budget, I primarily focused on smaller items such as those manufactured by Degenhart. However, mom's collection soon included Slag from all the major companies. Looking back, it is obvious that she had an eye for special pieces. Her collection included many items that are scarce today, such as a Purple Marble Raised Wing Swan by Westmoreland and a Jade Slag Large Rooster by Imperial.

I met Don Jennings in 1989, and he found all this glass collecting quite interesting. What first caught his attention were two pieces in my mom's collection – an Imperial Jade Slag Owl Covered Jar (see cover photo) and a Jade Slag Duck-on-Nest. Well, mom was going to make this irresistible for Don. She had been collecting glass for many years and it was time to start selling some things. One evening, while visiting my parents, Don purchased those two pieces of Imperial Jade Slag. Don had a new hobby and the start of our Imperial collection.

By 1990, Don and I had joined the National Imperial Glass Collectors Society and were attending our first convention. Soon, our collection also included Slag from Westmoreland, L. G. Wright, Fenton, and others. In 1994, the NIGCS convention featured Slag Glass by Imperial and our collection was used for a display. As part of a seminar that year, Don had researched through Imperial catalogs and price sheets and we developed a handout of all items that had been made in the various Slag colors. That research was the foundation for the development of this book.
Nathan Taves

Chapter 1

Definitions, History, and Values

Introduction

First, it is important to point out that Slag Glass and Marble Glass are two names for the same type of glass. More on that later.

As the title of this book implies, this is not an all-inclusive history of Slag Glass. Instead, it surveys Slag production by four American glass companies focusing primarily on the twenty-six year period from 1959 to 1985. These four companies include the Imperial Glass Corporation, Westmoreland Glass Company, L. G. Wright Glass Company, and the Fenton Art Glass Company. It was during these twenty-six years that, at one point or another, Slag Glass was an important part of each company's sales.

This is definitely not to say that Imperial, Wright, Westmoreland, and Fenton were the only ones making or selling Slag Glass or that all contemporary Slag production began in 1959 or ended in 1985. The Kanawha Glass Company, John E. Kemple Glassworks, Degenhart's Crystal Art Glass, Boyd's Crystal Art Glass, Mosser Glass, and the L. E. Smith Glass Company all made important contributions to the Slag production of that era. Chapter 6 provides examples of other companies that have made Slag Glass

The year 1959 was chosen as a starting point because that is when Imperial introduced Purple Slag, their first Slag color. For the record, it was not an immediate success. Fortunately, they persisted and eventually it began selling. What followed was a revival of Slag Glass popularity unknown since Victorian times. The ending year of 1985 sadly coincides with the period when both the Imperial and Westmoreland factories were liquidating their assets. Although Slag Glass was still being made at some factories, and it was still popular among many collectors, the heyday of its production was over.

The four companies represented here stand out because of their many wonderful mold designs, the quantity of items made, and the high quality of Slag production. Another way to look at this history is to realize that these four companies were competitors, and had much in common. Imperial, Wright, Westmoreland and Fenton each marketed their Slag production nationwide through regularly published catalogs, various showrooms, and sales representatives. The other companies mentioned above, who also made Slag, either marketed their wares more regionally or had a relatively small Slag production. Whereas Imperial, Westmoreland, and Fenton were all glass manufacturers on a large scale, Wright was a smaller operation and unique in that it did not produce its own glass; instead, Wright contracted others to make glass items for them. Fenton, Westmoreland, and Imperial all made Slag for Wright so that in documenting the Slag production of any one of those three, it is logical to review Wright as well.

Fenton is the only factory still in operation. Consequently, the molds of Imperial, Westmoreland, and Wright have been sold to other glass companies or organizations. Some of the molds continue to be in use. Much to the frustration of collectors, a few of the companies using these molds have not always removed the original factory's identifying mark. For collectors, the result has been a fair amount of confusion. Hopefully, this book will help sort out some of these problems. When trying to identify the maker of a particular piece, compare the color and/or mold mark with what has been documented in this book. If the color and mark do not match what has been listed for Imperial, Westmoreland or Wright, then it is reasonable to assume that you have one of the newer pieces. See Chapter 6 for photos of some of these newer items.

Defining Slag Glass

Some dealers and collectors refer to any opaque glass as Slag. For instance, it is common to see Chocolate Glass labeled as Chocolate Slag. Figure 1 shows three examples of Chocolate Glass. We define

Figure 1. Examples of Chocolate Glass: Cactus Pattern Covered Dish by Fenton, 2005; Fox Covered Dish by Westmoreland for the Levay Distributing Co., 1982; Robin Covered Dish by St. Clair, 1960s; Hen Covered Dish by Indiana Tumbler & Goblet Co. (often called Greentown Glass), c.1902.

Slag more specifically as the mixing of two or more distinct colors; therefore, colors such as Chocolate Glass or blue opaque glass would not qualify as Slag colors. To make a Slag color, usually white opaque Milk Glass is mixed or swirled together with a color such as amethyst, amber, or ruby. This produces a marble-like effect in the finished piece. All of the Slag colors by Imperial, Westmoreland, Wright, and Fenton were made using this method. In other opaque glass colors such as Chocolate Glass, there may be swirls and streaks with light and dark areas, but it is not the result of actually mixing two or more colors.

The Making of Slag

There are two basic ways in which colors are mixed to produce Slag Glass. The first uses two separate tanks of molten glass with different colors in each. The process begins with a small amount of one color ladled into the tank of the other, usually placing it within the confines of a ceramic ring floating on top of the molten glass. Next, a mixture of both colors is gathered from within this ring to make one molded item. Depending on the size of the piece being pressed, maybe one or maybe a few items could be made before more of the other color would have to be added to the ring. Therefore, making Slag glass requires this continuous process of adding one color to the tank of the other.

With all three of the glass factories represented in this book, each used this two tank method where Milk Glass was mixed with one other color, such as amethyst to make Purple Slag or amber to make Caramel Slag. Mixing a color (especially amethyst) with white is how most Slag Glass has been made dating back to its earliest years. During the 1950s until the 1970s, Milk Glass production was of primary importance to Westmoreland, Fenton, and Imperial. Westmoreland is famous for its Paneled Grape pattern and Fenton for its Hobnail pattern. Considering that Milk Glass was used to make most Slag Glass, it is not a complete coincidence that Slag Glass was made by the same factories that specialized in Milk Glass.

What makes the Slag Glass process unique are the artistic issues involved and the technical problem of fusing two glass colors. First, making a good-looking piece of Slag glass is more difficult than pressing a single color into a mold. In order for a glass factory to be profitable, it is important to remember that the final product must be handsome. Therefore, there is certain art and technical challenge in gathering and mixing two colors in such a way that the result is pleasing. The skill of these glass workers is evident in that consistently beautiful pieces were produced at these factories.

As for the technical issues, the mixing of any two colors has to survive the production process. This may sound simple, but different colors have different chemistries and characteristics. Unless the two colors are matched properly, particularly with their cooling rate, they will not fuse and the pressed piece will crack or break. In terms of production and labor costs, using two tanks of glass, an extra person to ladle the color of one tank into the other, and the risk of loosing pieces because of cracks and breakage, makes the production of Slag Glass a more expensive operation when compared to many other colors.

The second method of making Slag uses one tank instead of two. This approach is inevitably linked to Bernard C. Boyd who was the chemist for the Degenhart's Crystal Art Glass factory. Later, he and his family purchased the factory and operated it under the Boyd name. Years ago, Mr. Boyd described to us how he layered the various colors (usually two) in the tank and gathered some of each as a piece was being pressed. Often, one color would progress into another (with many slag variations along the way) during the course of a workday. Clearly, Mr. Boyd's knowledge of glass and its chemistry afforded him his great success with this single tank approach. It was rare that a batch did not produce beautiful results. Since his death in 1978, his son Bernard F., his daughter-in-law Sue, and grandson John, have continued this one tank tradition of making Slag.

A Very Condensed History of Slag

Production of pressed Slag glass dates back to the northeast part of England from the 1870s and continued to the early 1890s. The primary manufacturers were Sowerby's Ellison Street Glass Works, Henry Greener's Wear Flint Glass Works, and the George Davidson & Company, Ltd. In Figure 2, you will see a few examples of these pieces. Some pieces will have a British registry mark.[1]

By the 1880s, American companies were also making Slag, including Challinor, Taylor & Company in Tarentum, Pennsylvania; Atterbury & Company in Pittsburgh; and at the H. Northwood Company in Wheeling, West Virginia. By far, the predominant Slag color for both English and American items was purple, but other colors included blue, caramel or butterscotch, and green.[2] Figure 3 shows an assortment of American Slag glass from this era that ended soon after 1900.

It is also important to note that other American companies made Slag items throughout the 20th century. The Akro Agate Company started making marbles in 1911, and for almost the next forty years made many items including flowerpots and Slag children's dishes. Also, the L. J. Houze Convex Glass

Figure 2. Examples of Slag Glass by English companies, late 1800s.

Company made Slag candleholders, lamps, and gearshift knobs in the 1930s. In England, Davidson produced a Slag color called Cloud Glass in the 1920s and 1930s. See Chapter 6 for examples of Slag from these companies.

Figure 3. Examples of Slag Glass by American companies, late 1800s.

Slag, Marble, and Other Names

As stated at the beginning of this chapter, the names Slag and Marble are simply two names for exactly the same kind of glass. The term "slag" his-

torically refers to refuse separated from metal during the smelting process. Supposedly, this refuse was ground into sand and mixed with glass batches in the early years of making Slag Glass -- thus the use of the name.[3] The name Marble Glass seems self-explanatory in that the glass can look like a beautiful piece of marble stone with its many streaks and swirls.

Even though the name Slag is widely used today, that was not the case among Victorian era manufacturers. Those manufacturers preferred names like Mosaic or Variegated. By the time Ruth Webb Lee's well-known books on Victorian and early American pressed glass were published in the 1930s and 1940s, the name Marble Glass was in general use. However, she also documents it as being called Slag.[4]

When Slag Glass was reintroduced to the American market in 1959 by the Imperial Glass Company, the name Slag was chosen. The L. G. Wright Glass Company also used the name Slag. However, the Westmoreland Glass Company preferred the name Marble. The Fenton Art Glass Company has used both names. With all due respect to those using the name Marble Glass, we will use the name Slag Glass for all general use. This is consistent with what most collectors use today.

The other name associated with Slag is "End-of-Day," or as Imperial used for their Ruby Slag color, "End O' Day." No doubt, glass workers at times tried mixing different colors for the fun of it. However, considering the difficulty described above in making Slag glass, they probably had limited success. All Slag Glass by the factories represented in this book was the result of standard, deliberate, and systematic glass factory production. Even the whimsical items that you will see in this book that were obviously made for fun (such as a creamer being stretched into a vase) were not the result of randomly mixing two colors and hoping for the best. The name "End O' Day" as used by the Imperial factory, was a fanciful name for marketing purposes and selling glass rather than reflecting the reality of actual production.

Measurements and Sizes

All sizes are measured from the actual piece photographed to the nearest tenth of an inch. For those of you who have a manufacturer's catalogs or price sheets, you will immediately notice that our sizes will likely vary from what was published by the factory. Their measurements were almost always rounded to the nearest inch or half inch. Also, our sizes may vary from some of the pieces in your possession. With hand made glassware, this is inevitable and is especially noticeable with items like baskets or crimped and flared compotes.

Values

All values are for individual items unless they would normally be sold in pairs, such as with a cream and sugar set or candleholders - then the value listed is for a pair. It is also assumed that the piece is free of chips, cracks, or other flaws.

Our standard for assigning a value is the price that you would likely encounter in an antique shop or mall. It is important to remember that with Slag Glass, coloration and swirls of a particular piece can definitely influence price. Also, price is greatly dependent on the circumstance of the sale, such as the promotion and attendance at a live auction, all the quirky factors influencing Internet auctions, the region of the country, etc. For all of these reasons, prices are given as a range for catalog items. Prices for non-catalog items are given as a value with a plus sign (such as 200+), meaning that we think it is worth at least that amount or more depending on color, condition, etc. Ultimately, values are subjective. Therefore, please use the values listed in this book as a guide and only a guide. The authors assume no responsibility for any of the pricing information herein.

Overall, rarity affects price more than any other factor. Obviously, a non-catalog item, where probably only a very few were made, qualifies as very rare. For standard production items, rarity usually depends on how often and how long ago an item was made. If an item was made for only one year, then it will undoubtedly be relatively rare, and its value will reflect that.

As already mentioned, color also greatly affects value. The mix of the color or how the colors are blended is very important. Generally, good definition between the two colors in equal proportions seems to be the most desirable combination for many Slag collectors. With other glassware, there is typically not much variation in color from one piece to another; but with Slag, variation and differences are very much part of its appeal and desirability. Generally, Purple Slag commands higher prices simply because it is more popular than other colors; however, you will see in this book that there are many exceptions. Another factor that often affects price is whether any of the original factory stickers and labels are still intact. An original sticker is very important to some collectors.

Because of the way Slag Glass is made, cracking sometimes does occur. Typically cracks develop soon after an item is made due to stress within the glass. Two Slag colors are prone to cracks more than all the others -- Jade Slag by Imperial and Ruby Marble by Westmoreland. When buying an item in either of these colors, check carefully for cracks and buy or bid accordingly. If a piece is rare, a crack might be acceptable in order to acquire it for your collection. Unless the crack runs across or through the entire piece, usually the piece will not fall apart. Obviously, cracks are flaws that do adversely affect value.

Another issue that many of us encounter, or will someday, concerns determining values when selling a collection to a dealer for resale. Whether you are selling one piece at a time or a whole collection, please remember that the suggested values listed do not reflect what a dealer will realistically pay. The difference between the price a dealer will pay for a piece and the price at which that dealer will sell that piece, has to include a profit margin. Most collectors forget that a dealer is responsible for rent, hotel costs, gasoline, taxes, and a host of other overhead expenses.

Finishes: Glossy and Satin

Each of the companies in this book offered glassware, not necessarily Slag, in what is commonly called a satin finish. The term refers to a piece that has been either dipped in acid or sand blasted. This gives the item a matte or frosted finish instead of the glossy surface normally associated with glass. Imperial and Wright offered Slag items in both glossy and a satin finishes during certain years. With some exceptions, a satin finish can be added to glassware at any point after it has been made. When we were at the Wright company in the 1990s, they let us choose any animal covered dish to have acid dipped while we waited. Non-catalog Slag items with a satin finish can be found by Imperial, Fenton and Westmoreland. For the record, Imperial referred to Milk Glass satin items as "Doe Skin" (these pieces were both sand blasted and acid dipped), so occasionally collectors will use that term. Today, because of safety and environmental laws concerning the use of acids, factories such as Fenton exclusively use sand blasting techniques.

It should also be noted that having a satin finish can affect an item's value. If a piece was made for six years but only offered in satin for two years, it follows that the piece in satin will be harder to find than the same mold in a glossy finish and therefore more valuable. Also, keep in mind that because there was an extra charge for satin items, retailers may not have ordered them as readily thinking they would be harder to sell if they were more expensive.

Catalog Items and Non-catalog Items

We use the term "non-catalog" to mean an item made, for any reason, which is not documented in a factory catalog or price sheet. Often these will be feasibility or sample items used to evaluate what pieces would eventually be chosen for a catalog and regular production. Generally, only about a dozen or so were made of a particular mold. Over the years, we have found many pieces (many have been photographed for this book) that were undoubtedly made as feasibility or test items.

A non-catalog item also can refer to private production pieces. Typically, an individual, organization, or company would have a glass factory make an item for them. It might have been for a single color or it might have been for a series of different colors. A good example is the Venus Rising figure seen in Figure 43. This was originally a Cambridge mold, which was made by Imperial in various colors for Mirror Images.

Whimsies are another type of non-catalog item. Usually made for fun by glass workers, these include such items as creamers that were stretched into vases, and dishes that become baskets with the addition of an applied handle.

Bust-off items are non-catalog pieces associated with solid glass items such as animal figures. These are pressed upside-down with a base that is later removed. The bottom of the piece is then ground and sometimes polished. This base is called a bust-off, font, or break-off. Imperial and Westmoreland both made animals using this type of mold. Fenton continues to make animals this way. Happily for collectors, these animals can sometimes be found with the bust-off still attached. See Figures 44 and 477 for several examples.

Sometimes non-catalog items include a short production of several molds that are sold in the outlet or gift store at the factory. A good example is Fenton's "Almost Heaven" Blue Slag made in 1989. This color was sold exclusively in their gift shop. See Figure 544 for examples.

We have included many non-catalog items in this book; however, we know there are many more out there. Whatever the type, non-catalog items are a great source of fun for collectors. Happy hunting!

Mold Names and Other Terms

Collectors of other types of glass often use the mold number in referring to a particular piece. However, for whatever reason, Slag collectors do not typically rely on mold number to identify one piece from another. Slag collectors usually use a mold name instead. A problem then arises because older glass company catalogs were notorious for using rather generic mold names. For instance, there seem to be at least twenty Slag items in Imperial catalogs with the name "Box & Cover." Sometimes, a logical name was easily assigned to a mold and collectors long ago adopted it. In other situations, collectors have adopted various names resulting in a bit of confusion. For better or worse, and we certainly hope for better, we have assigned names for all molds. Sometimes we found a name associated with a particular mold dating back before Slag was made, so we used it. What should be obvious at this point is that the mold name you might run across in a catalog may not necessarily be the name we use.

Glass catalogs were also notorious for using different names in different catalogs for the same item. A puff box mold in one catalog is transformed into a jelly dish in another. Another example is where some companies use the name comport for a dish with a long-stemmed foot, other companies use the name compote, and others use both names interchangeably. For the record, Jim Measell, the author of several books on glass, has explained that "compote" refers to a concoction of stewed fruit and that a "comport" is actually the historically correct name for the dish that holds that food. However, compote seems to be the name most commonly used today for the stemmed dish, and so we have adopted it throughout this book. Regardless of the naming method, we hope the names we use offer consistency for the future.

Items Not Shown

We have documented some items that have not been photographed. You will see a text box describing them. Often, these pieces are quite rare and we simply were not able to photograph them. However, all such items have either been documented in a catalog, or we have personally seen the piece.

Reproductions

The topic of reproductions is a slippery one. When Imperial, Westmoreland, and L. G. Wright each closed, their glass molds were sold. When the molds were used by their new owners, the original mold marks were not always removed. This has caused a fair amount of distress among some collectors.

In 1976, when our first collecting habits began, discussions among dealers and collectors had been going on for years about how many molds and colors were being reproduced. Certain colors such as Carnival Glass, Milk Glass, and Chocolate Glass were definitely part of the controversy. For example, there were three 5" bird (robin) covered dishes that were a very close copy of a piece made by the Indiana Tumbler and Goblet Company of Greentown, Indiana, from around 1900. The three factories that had produced one of these bird covered dishes (dating back to the 1960s) included L. G. Wright Glass Company, Degenhart's Crystal Art Glass (the mold is now owned by Boyd's Crystal Art Glass), and St. Clair Glass (the mold was later sold to Summit Art Glass). Each factory was accused of reproducing the one from Greentown, causing collectors to be confused. In fact, one of the first pieces that found its way into our collection was an unmarked Chocolate Glass robin by St. Clair that was purchased as an authentic Greentown piece.

Today, decades later, a discussion concerning a reproduction such as the St. Clair version of a Greentown piece seems much less relevant. Books have documented the molds and colors of each factory and each bird mold was eventually marked. The reality is that many of the molds seen in this book are copies and variations of earlier molds. For example, almost all designs for the animal covered dishes are copies, to one degree or another, of earlier pieces by factories such as Atterbury & Company and the McKee Glass Company. The sticking point for many collectors is how the current owner of any given mold marks that item. To our knowledge, there are no copyright laws covering glass molds and so the discussion of reproductions will be ongoing -- at least for awhile. Hopefully, books will be written about the companies making the "reproductions" of recent years such that the controversy will become irrelevant much as it did with the robin covered dish.

Chapter 2

Imperial Glass Corporation

General History

The Imperial Glass Company dates back to 1901. Within a few years, a large factory was established in Bellaire, Ohio, and production started on a large number of tableware patterns in addition to other items such as bottles and light shades. Rather than building on the premise of starting small and growing bigger, they simply started very big. Their early catalogs included 150 pages or more, and by the end of 1906, the new Imperial factory had hundreds of employees. They started with crystal, using new designs in new molds, and were very successful. Often, the designs imitated Cut Glass. By 1909, iridescent (Carnival) glass was introduced. This started their history of producing decorative ware as well as utility items. Stretch Glass was introduce in 1916, Free Hand and Lead Lustre were part of 1920s, and many colored items arrived in the 1930s. Throughout these decades however, crystal tableware remained a stable part of their catalogs.

In 1931, the company reorganized into the Imperial Glass Corporation and ultimately survived financially difficult times. From early on, Imperial had decorated their crystal with hand engraving and sandblasting techniques, but in the early 1930s, they purchased a local glass decorating company, thereby enhancing this part of their operation. The 1930s also saw the birth of two of Imperial's most successful tabletop lines. The Cape Cod pattern started in 1931 and the Candlewick pattern around 1936. By the late 1940s, both patterns had become a major part of their production. Their success with these patterns is a pronounced part of their history. Today, there are probably more Candlewick collectors than any other glass tabletop pattern made during the twentieth century. Another pattern of importance was introduced in the 1930s called Lace Edge. Imperial produced Lace Edge items in many colors, including Slag pieces, for more that forty years.

Milk Glass became important in the 1950s and continued throughout the 1960s. This color included both tabletop pieces and decorative items. For our interests, it is important to note that many of the molds that were used in Milk Glass production were also used for Slag Glass. During the 1960s and 1970s, Imperial catalogs included Carnival Glass (reintroduced in 1961), Slag Glass, Candlewick, Lace Edge, Cape Cod, Crystal, and wide range of colored glassware including many high quality stemware items and serving pieces.

Two acquisitions were important to these later years. In 1958, Imperial purchased A. H. Heisey & Company, and in 1960, the Cambridge Glass Company. These two Ohio companies had produced elegant tabletop and decorative pieces. The use of molds from each of these companies can be seen in almost all subsequent catalogs. The Heisey animal molds are especially important to many collectors including Slag collectors.

In 1973, Lenox Incorporated, based in New Jersey, purchased Imperial. Overall, their emphasis was more on giftware and less on tabletop and utilitarian items. During the years of their ownership, an "L" for Lenox was often added to the traditional "IG" mold mark. Except for a few non-catalog items, no Slag items are marked with the "LIG" mold mark. In 1981, the factory was sold again to businessman Arthur Lorch who added an "A" in front of the "LIG" mold mark forming "ALIG." Most of the Caramel Slag items made in 1982 have this mark. The factory was sold one last time to Robert Stahl before it closed in 1984.[5]

Figure 4. Three Imperial mold marks found on Slag items.
  Left: IG mark found on most pieces of Slag Glass.
  Middle: LIG mark used during years of Lenox ownership, first used in 1977. All Slag items bearing this mark are non-catalog items.
  Right: ALIG mark used during years of Arthur Lorch ownership, June 1981 to September 1983.

Slag History at Imperial

Slag Glass production began at Imperial in 1959 primarily because of the initiative of one person – Carl W. Gustkey. However, the story actually begins with Lucile Kennedy. Lucile's title changed occasionally during her 40-year employment, but she basically assisted the president and sales staff. While on a business trip to Toledo, Ohio, she visited Betty Belknap. Her late husband, E. M. Belknap, had written an important book on Milk Glass that had been published in 1949 shortly before his death. During that visit with Mrs. Belknap, specifically while looking at old glass in her attic, she was shown "bushel baskets full of Slag Glass" and thought it was beautiful! With little doubt, what Lucile had seen were examples of Victorian era Slag pieces from the late 19th century.

Lucile Kennedy returned to work and told the president of Imperial Glass, Carl W. Gustkey, about the Slag Glass in Mrs. Belknap's attic. Mr. Gustkey was familiar with Slag Glass and its history and was enthusiastic about the possibility of producing it at Imperial. Imperial's chemist, Axel Ottoson, was responsible for developing the difficult glass formulations that would insure success. Eventually, nine molds were chosen to be made in Purple Slag. Unfortunately, they did not sell well at first. Instead of dropping the line, Mr. Gustkey wisely decided that more items should be added. As gift retailers will often testify, having enough pieces to make an impact on the customer is very important. Also, sometimes a new product simply need time to be noticed and appreciated. Mr. Gustkey was not only very well-liked and respected, he can be credited with much of Imperial's success during his twenty-seven years as chief executive. With his instinct for promoting Imperial wares, the backup of Lucile Kennedy, and Axel Ottoson to supervise the difficult chemistry involved, the rebirth of Slag Glass was underway.[6]

For the first few years, Imperial focused primarily on producing Purple Slag, but by 1964 an assortment of Caramel Slag was also being offered. This was followed by the introduction of Ruby Slag in 1969 and Jade Slag in 1975. All four colors were discontinued by 1977. In 1982, under the ownership of Arthur Lorch, Caramel Slag was produced for one year. Between 1959 and 1982, 19 total years, Imperial produced over 250 catalog items in one of their various colors. This was well over twice as many items offered as their nearest competitor -- Westmoreland.

If we compare this history with many instances where a glass factory discontinued a style or color after only a few years, the success of Slag Glass for Imperial was quite amazing. Purple Slag probably sold best overall, but Caramel Slag had to be a close second. Production problems kept Jade Slag in the line for only two years. Mixing the green and Milk Glass often resulted in the pieces cracking. Imperial made a few items in Blue Slag, primarily ashtrays in the mid-1960s and experimented with it again during the Lenox years, but decided against trying to market it.

Because of the way Slag is made, there is considerable color variation among pieces. This is true for Slag from any manufacturer. Sometimes, the formulations change over time and sometimes it is just the nature of a color to be inconsistent. Very early pieces of Purple Slag by Imperial will sometimes have streaks of crystal mixed with the amethyst and white. Some Caramel Slag is more gray than amber. Ruby,

because of its chemistry, can range from white mixed with dark red to shades of orange and yellow. When looking at the photographs in this book, you will see examples of many variations of Slag colors.

Figure 5.
   Left: Imperial color sample disk (non-catalog), Caramel Slag, 5-6" wide, $125+.
   Middle: Imperial tank sample (non-catalog), Ruby Slag, 2.3" long, $25+.
   Right: Imperial color sample disk (non-catalog), Purple Slag, 5-6" wide, $125+.

Mold Numbers

You will notice in the photo captions for Imperial that often two mold numbers are listed. The first is an older numbering system that Imperial had used for many years. Sometimes this referred to a pattern number and sometimes to an individual mold. The second number references the system initiated in the 1974-75 catalog after Lenox bought the Imperial factory. This is a five-digit number with Slag items starting with "43."

Mold Marks, Factory Stickers, and Point of Purchase Tags

Slag Glass by Imperial can be found with several mold marks. Previously mentioned was the "IG" mark that was used starting in the 1950s, the "LIG" mark designating the years that Lenox owned the factory, and the "ALIG" mark used when Arthur Lorch was owner. Other marks include an "H" in a diamond that had been used by Heisey. After Imperial purchased Heisey, sometimes their mark was left on temporarily if the mold was being tested in a particular color. A few items in Caramel Slag can be found this way. Only the Colonial 2-Handled Toothpick Holder (#600) was made using Imperial's Iron Cross mark, but it is often too faint to detect.

The Imperial factory sticker used on their Slag items is oval-shaped with blue and silver colors reading "Hand Crafted Imperial USA." See Figure 5 for an example. The various colors sometimes had their own square stickers saying "Purple Slag Glass Circa 1850 By Imperial" or "Caramel Slag End Of Day Glass By Imperial." The one for Ruby Slag read "Olden End O' Day Glass by Imperial." Ware stickers included the company name on the top in red followed by the mold number and a short description but did not include a retail price. Hangtags or point of purchase tags were sometimes included with an item. Purple, Ruby, and Caramel each had their own tag that included a brief history of Slag. See Figure 6 for examples.

Figure 6. Examples of three hangtags or point of purchase tags used with Imperial Slag items:
  Top: Purple Slag tag, front and back.
  Middle: Caramel Slag tag, front and back.
  Bottom: Ruby Slag tag, front and back.

Private Productions

One private production project needs special attention. In 1963, Sears, Roebuck and Company worked with Vincent Price (the actor), his wife Mary, and a group of buyers to select and reproduce home furnishing items that were historically significant. 250 pieces, called the *National Treasures Collection,* were chosen to represent American's heritage spanning the years from 1607 to 1900. Imperial made eleven items for Sears of which three are of special interest to Slag collectors. The Owl Covered Jar (#800) and the Owl Cream & Sugar Set (#335) were made in Purple Slag representing both the original molds and Slag color made by factories such as Challinor, Taylor and Company of Pittsburgh during the Victorian era. Records show that only about 360 sets were made and sometimes are found with bright orange eyes attached instead of the amber that was typically used.[7] See Figure 218 for examples.

Two other private production pieces were for Mirror Images of Lansing, Michigan, and for PeeGee Glass Company of Fort Wayne, Indiana. Mirror Images used a mold called Venus Rising from Imperial and had it pressed in Caramel Slag in 1982. See Figure 43. Mirror Images called the color Caramelita. Using a mold of their own design, PeeGee Glass had Imperial make their Mouse Lovers also in Caramel Slag in 1982. See Figure 38. For both of these companies, these pieces were a part of a twelve color series.

Figure 9. Duck Covered Dish, #823, 5.5" wide, Purple Slag, 1959-60, not marked, $200-225.

Figure 7. Squirrel Covered Dish, #821, 5.5" wide, Purple Slag, 1959-60, not marked, $225-250.

Figure 10. Dog Covered Dish, #822 or 43199, 5.5" wide, Purple Slag, 1959-1960, not marked, $200-225.

Figure 8. Bee Covered Dish, #825, 5.5" wide, Purple Slag, 1959-70, not marked or IG mark, $100-120.

Figure 11. Dog Covered Dish, #822 or 43199, 5.5" wide, Caramel Slag, 1982, ALIG mark, $115-135; also shown is a whimsey (non-catalog) made from the finial, $75+.

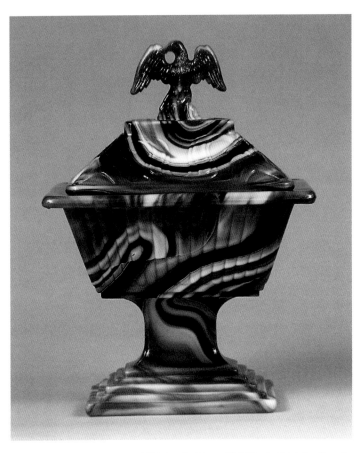

Figure 12. Eagle Covered Dish, #461 or 43879, 8.6" high, Purple Slag, 1969-73, satin 1973, IG mark, $150-175.

Figure 14. Lion Covered Dish, #159 or 43873, 7.5" long, Purple Slag, 1964-73, satin 1973, IG mark, $175-185.

Figure 13. Eagle Covered Dish, #461 or 43879, 8.6" high, Caramel Slag, 1969-73, satin 1973, IG mark, $110-130.

Figure 15. Lion Covered Dish, #159 or 43873, 7.5" long, Caramel Slag, 1970-73, satin 1973, IG mark, $150-175.

Figure 16. Rabbit Covered Dish, #157, 7.5" long, Purple Slag, 1964-67, IG mark, $550-600.

Figure 18. Rooster Covered Dish, #158 or 43870, 7.5" long, Jade Slag, 1975-76, satin 1975-76, IG mark, $500-550.

Figure 17. Rooster Covered Dish, #158 or 43870, 7.5" long, Caramel Slag, 1970-76, satin 1973-76, IG mark, $140-160.

Figure 19. Rooster Covered Dish, #158 or 43870, 7.5" long, Purple Slag, 1964-1974, satin 1973-74, IG mark, $160-180.

Figure 20. Rooster Holder, #459 or 43639, 4.2" high, IG mark:
  Left: Ruby Slag, 1971-75, satin 1971-75, $45-50.
  Middle: Jade Slag, 1975, satin 1975, $75-85.
  Right: Caramel Slag, 1975, satin 1975, $65-75.

Figure 21. Duck-on-Nest, #146 or 43920, 4.4" long, IG mark:
  Left: Jade Slag, 1975-76, satin 1975-76, $70-80.
  Middle: Caramel Slag, 1971-76, satin 1973-76, $35-40.
  Right: Purple Slag, 1971-74, satin 1973-74, $50-60.

Below:
Figure 22. Owl Covered Jar, #800 or 43900, 6.5" high, IG mark:
  Left: Purple Slag, 1970-74, satin 1973-74, $80-90.
  Middle: Jade Slag, 1975-76, satin 1975-76, $100-110.
  Right: Caramel Slag, 1970-76, satin 1973-76, $55-65.

Figure 23.
  Left: Standard IG mark on Purple Slag Owl Covered Jar, #800.
  Right: Owl Covered Jar, #800, private production (non-catalog), 6.5" high, Purple Slag, c.1965, marked SVPNT (Sears Vincent Price National Treasures) for a special promotion by Sears, Roebuck and Company. About 360 made, eye color can be amber or bright orange (see Figure 218), $250+.

Figure 24. Small Open Swan (Mint Whimsy), #147 or 43930, 5.0" long:
Left: Caramel Slag, 1970-76, satin 1973-76, IG mark, $30-35.
Middle: Purple Slag, 1960-74, satin 1973-74, not marked or IG mark, $35-40.
Right: Jade Slag, 1975-76, satin 1975-76, IG mark, $50-60.

Figure 25. Large Open Swan, #400 or 43932, 9.5" long, Jade Slag, 1975, satin 1975, IG mark, $185-210.

Figure 26. Large Open Swan, #400 or 43932, 9.5" long, Purple Slag, 1969-74, satin 1973-74, IG mark, $90-100.

Figure 27. Large Open Swan, #400 or 43932, 9.5" long, Caramel Slag, 1969-75, satin 1973-75, IG mark, $80-90.

Figure 28.
  Left: Bull Dog Parlour Pup, #5/1 or 43943, 3.0" high, Caramel Slag, 1969-75, not marked or IG mark, $35-40.
  Right: Scottie Dog Parlour Pup, #5/2, 2.7" high, Caramel Slag, 1969-1970, not marked or IG mark, $70-80.

Figure 29.
  Left: Terrier (tongue out) Parlour Pup, #5/3, 3.5" high, Caramel Slag, 1969-70, not marked or IG mark, $70-80.
  Right: Terrier (tail up) Parlour Pup, #5/4 or 43944, 3.1" high, Caramel Slag, 1969-1975, not marked or IG mark, $35-40.

Figure 30.
  Left: Champ Terrier (Airedale), #14 or 43947, 6.0" high, Caramel Slag, 1969-1973, Heisey mold, not marked or IG mark, $125-150.
  Right: Scotty Champ (Scottie Dog), #11, 4.8" long, Caramel Slag, 1969-1970, Heisey mold, not marked or IG mark, $170-195.

Figure 31. Scottie Dog Bookends, #1128 or 43951, 6.2" high, Caramel Slag, 1982, Cambridge mold, ALIG mark, $550-650 pair. Good color and match greatly effects value.

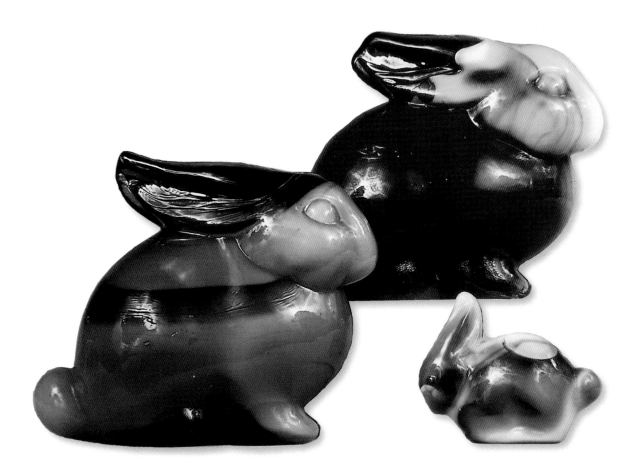

Figure 32.
   Left: Mother Rabbit, #1, 4.6" high, Nut Brown Slag (non-catalog), c.1978, Heisey mold, IG mark, $1000+.
   Middle: Mother Rabbit, #1, 4.6" high, Ruby Slag (non-catalog), date unknown, Heisey mold, IG mark, $1000+.
   Right: Bunny, #2 or 43935, 2.5" high, Caramel Slag, 1982, Heisey mold, ALIG mark, $55-65.

Figure 33.
   Left: Standing Colt, #12/3 or 43946, 5.0" high, Caramel Slag, 1969-76, Heisey mold, IG mark, $35-40.
   Middle: Kicking Colt, #12/4, 4.2" high, Caramel Slag, 1969-70, Heisey mold, IG mark, $150-175.
   Right: Balking Colt (Rearing Colt), #12/2, 3.7" high, Caramel Slag, 1969-70, Heisey mold, not marked or IG mark, $150-175.

Figure 34.
   Left: Donkey (Wild Jack), #1 or 43941, 6.5" high, Caramel Slag, 1969-76, Heisey mold, not marked or IG mark, $50-55.
   Right: Pony Stallion (Oscar or Plug Horse), #12/1 or 43945, 4.0" high, Caramel Slag, 1969-76, Heisey mold, IG mark, $50-55.

Figure 35.
  Left: Wings Up Mallard, #9/1 or 43939, 6.5" high, Caramel Slag, 1969-76, Heisey mold, not marked or IG mark, $45-50.
  Middle: Wings Down Mallard, #9/3, 5.0" high, Caramel Slag, 1969-70, Heisey mold, not marked or IG mark, $275-300.
  Right: Wings Half Mallard, #9/2 or 43940, 5.0" high, Caramel Slag, 1969-76, Heisey mold, not marked or IG mark, $40-45.

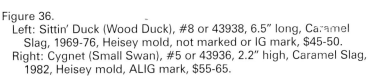

Figure 36.
  Left: Sittin' Duck (Wood Duck), #8 or 43938, 6.5" long, Caramel Slag, 1969-76, Heisey mold, not marked or IG mark, $45-50.
  Right: Cygnet (Small Swan), #5 or 43936, 2.2" high, Caramel Slag, 1982, Heisey mold, ALIG mark, $55-65.

Figure 37. Hoot (less) Owl, #18 or 43948, 3.7" high, Caramel Slag, 1969-76, not marked or IG mark, $35-40.

Figure 38.
  Left: Scolding Bird, #10 or 43931, 5.2" high, Caramel Slag, 1982, ALIG mark, $145-165.
  Right: Mouse Lovers, private production (non-catalog) for PeeGee Glass, 3.0" high, Caramel Slag, 1982, IG mark, $30+.

Figure 39. Tiger Paperweight, #103 or 43957, 8.0" long, Caramel Slag, 1982, Heisey mold, ALIG mark, $165-185.

Figure 40.
   Left: Eminent (Middle) Elephant, #2 or 43942, 6.3" long, Caramel Slag, 1969-76, Heisey mold, not marked or IG mark, $50-55.
   Right: Small Elephant, #3 or 43933, 4.7" high, Caramel Slag, Heisey mold, ALIG mark, $85-95.

Figure 41. Eminent Elephant, #2 or 43942, 6.3" long Caramel Slag:
   Left: standard catalog piece. Notice the trunk angle differs from the example in Figure 40 due to how the bottom was ground, $50-55.
   Right: Notice the hole drilled through the trunk curl (non-catalog), $100+.

Figure 42. Woodchuck (Marmota Sentinel), #19 or 43946, 4.5" high, Caramel Slag, 1969-75, not marked or IG mark, $40-45.

Figure 43.
  Left: Venus Rising (Bashful Charlotte), 6.6" high, private production (non-catalog) for Mirror Images, Caramel Slag, their color name was Caramelita, 1981, satin 1981, Cambridge mold, IG mark, $45+.
  Right: Minuet Girl, #1 or 43835, 4.5" high, Caramel Slag, 1982, Heisey mold, ALIG mark, $50-60.

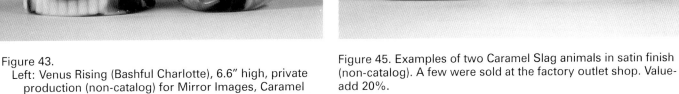

Figure 45. Examples of two Caramel Slag animals in satin finish (non-catalog). A few were sold at the factory outlet shop. Value-add 20%.

Figure 44. Examples of Caramel Slag animals on bust-offs (non-catalog). Depending on animal and condition, $150-400.

Figure 46.
  Left: Heart Ashtray (Pin Dish), #294 or 43854, 4.3" long, Caramel Slag (non-catalog), date unknown, IG mark, $200+.
  Right: Heart Ashtray (Pin Dish), #294 or 43854, 4.3" long, Ruby Slag, 1969-76, satin 1969-76, IG mark, $25-30.

Figure 47. Paperweight whimsey (non-catalog) from Heart Ashtray (#294), Ruby Slag, 5.0" wide, date unknown, not marked, $40+.

Figure 48. Hambone Ashtray, #1956 or 43865, 8.0" long, Cambridge mold, not marked:
  Left: Ruby Slag, 1976, satin 1976, $35-40.
  Right: Jade Slag, 1976, satin 1976, $50-55.

Figure 49. Hambone Ashtray, #1956 or 43865, 8.0" long, Cambridge mold, not marked:
  Left: Caramel Slag, 1976, satin 1976, $35-40.
  Right: Purple Slag, 1962-67, $40-45.

Figure 50. Olde Jamestowne Square Ashtray, #1608/1 or 43858, 5.7-6.0" wide, not marked, may be found with a large paper label on the underside:
    Left: Blue Slag, 1963, $50-60.
    Middle: Caramel Slag, 1963-76, satin 1973-76, $20-25.
    Right: Ruby Slag, 1969-1976, satin 1969-76, $20-25.

Figure 51. Olde Jamestowne Square Ashtray, #1608/1 or 43858, 5.7-6.0" wide, not marked, may be found with a large paper label on the underside:
    Left: Jade Slag, 1975-76, satin 1975-76, $25-30.
    Right: Green Slag, 1963, $20-25.

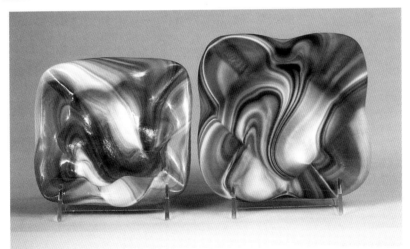

Figure 52.
    Left: Olde Jamestowne Square Ashtray with six-point center (non-catalog), mold number unknown, 5.6" wide, Purple Slag, date unknown, not marked, $75+.
    Right: Olde Jamestowne Square Ashtray, #1608/1 or 43858, 5.7-6.0" wide, Purple Slag, 1962-74, satin 1973-74, not marked, may be found with a large paper label on the underside, $25-30.

Figure 53.
    Left: Large Square Ashtray, #1489, 7.0" wide, Purple Slag, 1959-60, not marked, $90-100.
    Right: Small Square Ashtray, #1489, 4.6" wide, Purple Slag, 1960-67, not marked, $25-30.

Figure 54. Olde Jamestowne
Round Ashtray (Bowl), #1605 or
43681, 7.4" wide, not marked:
  Left: Caramel Slag, 1964-67 &
    1975, satin 1975, $25-30.
  Right: Purple Slag, 1965-67,
    $75-100.

Figure 55. Olde Jamestowne
Round Ashtray (Bowl), #1605 or
43681, 7.4" wide, not marked:
  Left: Ruby Slag, 1975-76, satin
    1975-76, $40-45.
  Right: Jade Slag, 1966 & 1975,
    satin 1975, $45-50.

Figure 56. Olde Jamestowne
Round Ashtray (Bowl), #1605
or 43681, 7.4" wide, Blue Slag,
c.1963, not marked, $60-75.

Figure 57.
  Left: Candlewick Ashtray,
    #400/150, 5.9" wide, Caramel
    Slag (non-catalog), c.1965, not
    marked, $125+.
  Right: Dog Collar (Top Dawg)
    Ashtray, #43863, 5.2" wide,
    Caramel Slag, 1982, ALIG
    mark, $75-85.

Figure 58.
Left: Boudoir Ashtray, #150, 4.3" wide, Purple Slag, 1962-67, IG mark, $35-40.
Right: Boudoir Ashtray with brass handle whimsey (non-catalog) from mold #150, 4.3"
wide, Purple Slag, date unknown, not marked, $75+.

Figure 59.
Left: Cape Cod Lighter, #1602, 4.5" high, Purple Slag, 1962-67,
not marked, $55-65.
Right: Atlantis (Shell) Ashtray, #291, 4.5" wide, Purple Slag,
1961-67, IG mark, $25-30.

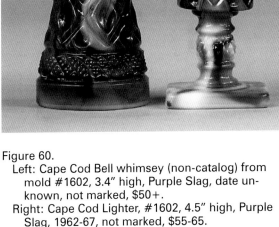

Figure 60.
Left: Cape Cod Bell whimsey (non-catalog) from
mold #1602, 3.4" high, Purple Slag, date un-
known, not marked, $50+.
Right: Cape Cod Lighter, #1602, 4.5" high, Purple
Slag, 1962-67, not marked, $55-65.

Figure 61. Contour Ashtray, mold number
unknown, 6.7" wide, Purple Slag (non-catalog), date unknown, not marked, $100+.
Although this is a Duncan & Miller mold, it
was purchased at the Imperial factory outlet
store. Assumed to be made by Imperial.

Figure 62. Chevron Basket, #156 or 43642, 5.3" wide, IG mark:
  Left: Ruby Slag, 1969-76, satin 1969-76, $40-45.
  Right: Purple Slag, 1969-74, satin 1973-74, $50-55.

Figure 63. Chevron Basket, #156 or 43642, 5.3" wide, IG mark:
  Left: Caramel Slag, 1969-76, satin 1973-76, $40-45.
  Right: Jade Slag, 1975-76, satin 1975-76, $60-70.

Figure 65. Miniature Sawtooth Basket, #475, 5.2" high, Ruby Slag, 1969-70, satin 1969-70, IG mark, $50-60.

Figure 64. Chevron Basket whimsey (non-catalog) from mold #156, 8.4" long, Caramel Slag, IG mark, $300+.

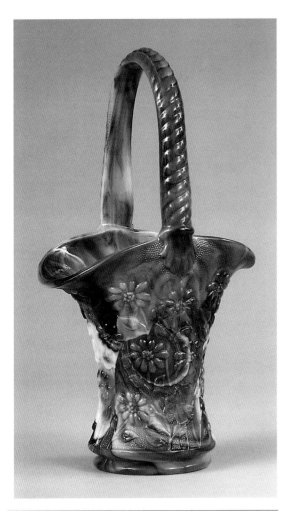

Figure 66. Daisy Basket, #40 or 43644, 9.7" high, Purple Slag, 1960-61, not marked, $200-225.

Figure 68. Smooth Basket, #300, 9.9" high, Ruby Slag, 1969-73, satin 1969-73, IG mark, $80-90.

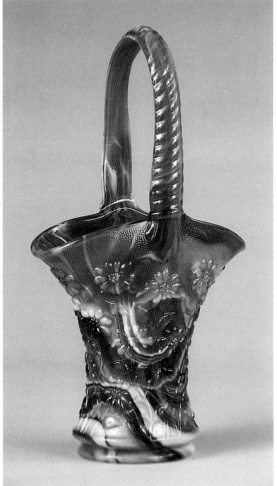

Figure 67. Daisy Basket, #40 or 43644, 9.7" high, Caramel Slag, 1964-73, satin 1973, IG mark, $75-85.

Figure 69. Smooth Basket with Milk Glass handle (non-catalog) from mold #300, 8.2" high, Ruby Slag, date unknown, IG mark, $200+.

Figure 70. Windmill Basket, crimped, #514 or 43641, 9.0" wide, Caramel Slag, 1982, ALIG mark, $125-150.

Figure 71. Windmill Basket, flared (non-catalog), #514 or 43641, 10.4" wide, Caramel Slag, c.1982, ALIG mark, $200+.

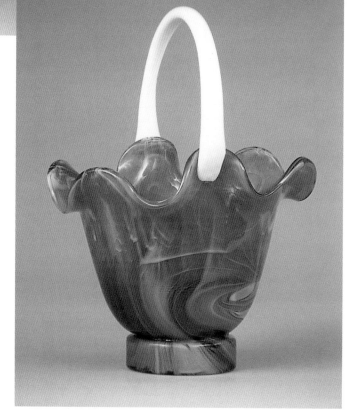

Figure 72. Windmill Basket, flared with Caramel Slag handle (non-catalog), #514 or 43641, 9.6" wide, Caramel Slag, c.1982, ALIG mark, $300+.

Figure 73. Wavy Edge Basket, mold number unknown, 9.4" high, Caramel Slag (non-catalog), c.1982, ALIG mark, $400+.

Figure 74. Dresden Girl Bell, #1123 or 43846, 7.8" high, Caramel Slag, 1982, Cambridge mold, ALIG mark, $90-100.

Figure 76. Smooth Bell, #720 or 43842, 5.5" high, not marked:
Left: Purple Slag, 1971-74, satin 1973-74, $60-70.
Right: Caramel Slag, 1971-76, satin 1973-76, $45-50.

Figure 75. Smooth Bell, #720 or 43842, 5.5" high, not marked:
Left: Ruby Slag, 1971-76, satin 1971-76, $50-55.
Right: Jade Slag, 1975-76, satin 1975-76, $65-75.

Figure 77.
Left: Smooth Bell, #720 or 43842, 5.5" high, Purple Slag, 1971-74, satin 1973-74, not marked, $60-70.
Right: Cup whimsey with chrome base (non-catalog) from Smooth Bell (#720), 3.1" high, Purple Slag, date unknown, not marked, $75+.

Figure 78. 3-Toed Rose Bowl, crimped, #74C or 43693, 8.2" wide, Purple Slag, 1969-74, satin 1973-74, IG mark, $60-75.

Figure 80. 3-Toed Rose Bowl, crimped, #74C or 43693, 8.2" wide, Jade Slag, 1975-76, satin 1975-76, IG mark, $70-80.

Figure 79. 3-Toed Rose Bowl, crimped, #74C or 43693, 8.2" wide, Caramel Slag, 1969-76, satin 1973-76, IG mark, $45-50.

Figure 81. 3-Toed Rose Bowl, crimped, #74C or 43693, 8.2" wide, Blue Slag (non-catalog), date unknown, LIG mark, $450+.

Figure 82. Rose Bowl, crimped, #62C or 43699, 9.2" wide, Ruby Slag, 1969-76, satin 1969-76, IG mark, $50-55.

Figure 84. Rose Bowl, crimped, #62C or 43699, 9.2" wide, Caramel Slag, 1974-76, satin 1974-76, IG mark, $45-50.

Figure 83. Rose Bowl, crimped, #62C or 43699, 9.2" wide, Purple Slag, 1960-74, satin 1973-74, IG mark, $55-65.

Figure 85. Rose Bowl, crimped, #62C or 43699, 9.2" wide, Jade Slag, 1975-76, satin 1975-76, IG mark, $65-75.

Figure 86. Rose Bowl, not crimped, #62C or 43699, 7.4" wide, Ruby Slag (non-catalog), date unknown, IG mark, $400+.

Figure 88. 3-Toed Rose Bowl, strait-sided, #43685, 7.5" wide, Caramel Slag (non-catalog), date unknown, not marked, $300+.

Figure 87. Rose Bowl, three-fold crimp (non-catalog) from mold #62C, 8.8" wide, Purple Slag, date unknown, IG mark, $325+.

Figure 89. Beaded Ribbed Oval Bowl, #463, 9.8" long, Caramel Slag (non-catalog), c.1982, ALIG mark, $400+.

Figure 90. Grape Bowl, crimped, #47C or 43696, 9.8" wide, Ruby Slag, 1969-73, satin 1969-73, IG mark, $65-75.

Figure 92. Windmill Bowl, crimped, stippled on back, #52C or 43691, 8.0" wide, Caramel Slag, 1964-73, satin 1973, IG mark, $45-50.

Figure 91. Grape Bowl, crimped, #47C or 43696, 9.8" wide, Caramel Slag, 1982, ALIG mark, $65-75. Can also be found as a non-catalog item with LIG mark, date unknown.

Figure 93. Windmill Bowl, crimped, thin panels on back, #514C or 43695, 9.0" wide, Caramel Slag, 1982, ALIG mark, $50-55.

Figure 94. Fancy Flowers Footed Bowl, #737A or 43698, 8.7" wide, Purple Slag, 1971-73, satin 1973, IG mark, $80-90.

Figure 96. Fancy Flowers Footed Bowl, #737A or 43698, 8.7" wide, Ruby Slag, 1974-75, satin 1974-75, IG mark, $70-80.

Figure 95. Fancy Flowers Footed Bowl, #737A or 43698, 8.7" wide, Caramel Slag, 1971-73, satin 1973, IG mark, $70-80.

Figure 097. Wheels Bowl, #43554, 4.7" wide, Blue Slag (non-catalog), date unknown, LIG mark, $350+.

Figure 98. Large Salad Bowl, 11.2" wide, #602, Jade Slag, 1966-67, not marked, may be found with large round paper label on bottom, $1000+.

Figure 99. Large Salad Bowl, #602, 11.2" wide, Caramel Slag, 1966-67, not marked, may be found with large round paper label on bottom, $350-400.

Figure 100. Small Salad Bowl, #602, 6.4" wide, not marked, may be found with large round paper label on bottom:
   Left: Caramel Slag, 1966-67, $100-125.
   Right: Jade Slag, 1966-67, $250-300.

Figure 101. Small Salad Bowl, #602, showing paper label on bottom.

Figure 102. Large Salad Bowl, mold number unknown, 11.9" wide, Caramel Slag (non-catalog), date unknown, not marked, $900+.

Figure 103. Small Salad Bowl, mold number unknown, 6.7" wide, Caramel Slag (non-catalog), date unknown, not marked, $250+.

Figure 104. Large Pointed Hobnail Bowl, #642, 10.5" wide, Purple Slag, 1960-61, not marked, $275-325.

Figure 105.
Left: Medium Pointed Hobnail Bowl, #641, 8.5" wide, Purple Slag, 1961-70, not marked, $75-95.
Right: Small Pointed Hobnail Bowl, #640, 4.6" wide, Purple Slag, 1969-70, IG mark, $75-85.

Figure 106. Lace Edge Flower Bowl, #7802K, 5.1" wide, Purple Slag (non-catalog), date unknown, IG mark, $350+.

Figure 107. Open Edge Atterbury Bowl, #159/1, 7.5" long, Purple Slag, 1961-68, IG mark, $60-70.

Figure 108. Lace Edge Bowl, #7808F, 10.7" wide, Purple Slag (non-catalog), date unknown, not marked, $350+.

Figure 109. Cut Lace Edge Shallow Dish (front & back), #363F, 6.1" wide, Purple Slag, 1961-68, IG mark, $70-80.

Figure 110. Lace Edge Punch Bowl (shown with one cup & ladle), #780, 13.8" wide, Purple Slag, 1962-63, not marked, $3500+ for 14-piece set.

Figure 111. Heart Dish, #312/1, 5.8" long, Purple Slag, 1962-67, not marked, $60-70.

Figure 112. 2-Handled Clothes Basket Bowl, #456, 7.4" long, Purple Slag, 1961, IG mark, $175-200.

Figure 113. Tulip & Cane Nut (Mint) Dish, #9/1, 4.0" wide, Purple Slag, 1962-67, not marked, $65-75.

Figure 114. Pansy Nappy, #478 or 43574, 5.4" wide, IG mark:
   Left: Ruby Slag, 1975-76, satin 1975-76, $45-50.
   Middle: Jade Slag, 1975-76, satin 1975-76, $50-55.
   Right: Caramel Slag, 1975-76, satin 1975-76, $35-40.

Figure 115. Grape Nappy, #851 or 43576, 5.4" wide:
   Left: Ruby Slag, 1972-75, satin 1972-75, IG mark, $45-50.
   Right: Caramel Slag (non-catalog), date unknown, LIG mark, $200+.

Figure 116.
   Left: Shell Tray, #199 or 43580, 7.6" wide, Caramel Slag, 1982, ALIG mark, $50-60.
   Right: Shell Dish, #297, 7.3" wide, Caramel Slag, 1964-67, not marked, $40-45.

Figure 117. Duo Shell Tidbit, wrought iron stand, mold #297, 10.3" long, Caramel Slag (non-catalog), date unknown, not marked, $200+.

Figure 118. Candlewick Oval Divided Relish, #400/256, 11.1" long, Caramel Slag (non-catalog), c.1965, not marked, $275+.

Figure 119. Candlewick 2-Handled Bowl, #400/52B, 7.0" long, Caramel Slag (non-catalog), c.1965, not marked, $225+.

Figure 120. Candlewick Heart Dish, #400/174, 6.5" wide, Caramel Slag (non-catalog), c.1965, not marked, $175+.

Figure 121. Candlewick 3-Toed Bowl, #400/182, 8.5" long, Caramel Slag (non-catalog), c.1965, not marked, $700+.

Not Shown: Candlewick 3-Toed Bowl, #400/183, 6" wide, Caramel Slag (non-catalog), c.1965, not marked, $850+.

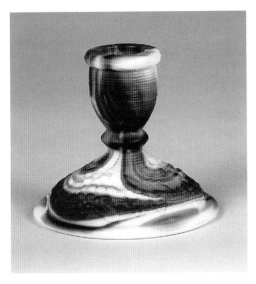

Figure 122. Grape Candleholder, #880 or 43782, 3.4" high, Ruby Slag, 1969-73, satin 1969-73, IG mark, $50-55 pair.

Figure 124. Rose Candleholder, #160 or 43784, 3.4" high, IG mark:
   Left: Purple Slag, 1974, satin 1974, $60-65 pair.
   Right: Caramel Slag, 1974-75, satin 1974-75, $45-50 pair.

Figure 123. Rose Candleholder, #160 or 43784, 3.4" high, IG mark:
   Left: Ruby Slag, 1971-75, satin 1971-75, $55-60 pair.
   Right: Jade Slag, 1975, satin 1975, $80-90 pair.

Figure 125. Pointed Hobnail Candleholder, #643, 4.3" wide, Nut Brown Slag (non-catalog), date unknown, IG mark, $275+ each.

Figure 126. Handled Candleholder (front & back), #81, 6.6" long, Purple Slag, 1962 (six months only), IG mark, $800+ each.

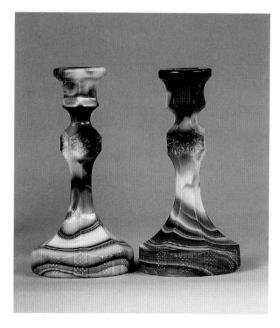

Figure 127. Six-sided Candleholder, #352 or 43790, 7.5" high, not marked:
  Left: Purple Slag, 1971-73, satin 1973, $80-90 pair.
  Right: Caramel Slag, 1971-73, satin 1973, $70-80 pair.

Figure 128.
  Left: Dolphin Candleholder, #779, 5.0" high, Caramel Slag, 1964-67, IG mark, $70-80 pair.
  Right: Cane Candleholder, #671 or 43794, 6.9" high, Caramel Slag, 1982, ALIG mark, $90-100 pair.

Figure 129. Atterbury (Vertical Rib) Candleholder, #330, 7.3" high, Purple Slag, 1960 (six months only), not marked, $500-600 pair.

Figure 131. Drilling a hole in the bottom of Tulip & Cane Nut Dish, mold #9/1, on right, made Bundling Lamp shade on left.

Figure 130. Bundling Lamp, Tulip & Cane pattern, #9, 8.8" high, Purple Slag, 1962-64, not marked, $400-450.

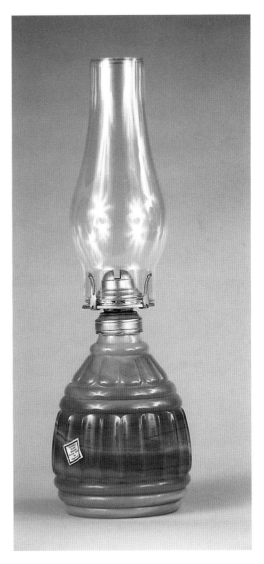

Figure 132. Cask Bottle Lamp (non-catalog) from mold #1, 15.5" high, Purple Slag, date unknown, not marked, $750+.

Figure 133. Thumbprint Compote, #973, 4.4" high, Purple Slag, 1961-68, not marked, $70-80.

Figure 135. Atterbury Footed Bowl (Vertical Ribbed Compote), #203F, 7.7" wide, Purple Slag, 1959-60, IG mark, $200-225.

Figure 134. Hobnail Compote, #66C, 5.2" high, Purple Slag (non-catalog), date unknown, IG mark, $550+.

Figure 136. Lace Edge 4-Toed Compote, #274C, 4.5" high, Purple Slag, 1960-67, IG mark, $70-80.

Figure 137. Octagon Compote, crimped, #5930 or 43729, 4.5" high, not marked:
Left: Jade Slag, 1975, satin 1975, $55-60.
Middle: Caramel Slag, 1974-75, satin 1974-75, $35-40.
Right: Purple Slag, 1961-74, satin 1973-74, $45-50.

Figure 138. Grape (Hexagon) Compote, crimped, #727C or 43723, 4.0" high, Jade Slag, 1975, satin 1975, IG mark $75-85.

Figure 139. Grape (Hexagon) Compote, crimped, #727C or 43723, 4" high, Purple Slag, 1969-74, satin 1973-74, IG mark, $55-60.

Figure 140. Grape (Hexagon) Compote, crimped, #727C or 43723, 4" high, Caramel Slag, 1969-75, satin 1973-75, IG mark, $40-45.

Figure 141. Smooth Compote, crimped, #431C, 6.3" high, Ruby Slag, 1969-73, satin 1969-73, IG mark, $45-50.

Figure 143. Waverly Oval Compote, #1519/45, 6.1" high, Caramel Slag, 1964-70, Heisey mold, not marked or Heisey mark, $45-50.

Figure 142. Saddle (Zipper) Compote, #48, 7.0" high, Caramel Slag, 1964-68, IG mark, $90-100.

Figure 144. Dolphin Compote, #778, 7.5" high, Caramel Slag, 1964-67, IG mark, $90-100.

Figure 145. Two Ball Compote, #761 or 43721, Caramel Slag, 1982, ALIG mark:
　　Left: crimped (non-catalog), 5.1" high, $65+.
　　Right: as shown in catalog, 5.2" high, $45-50.

Figure 146. Chroma Compote, #123 or 43738, Caramel Slag, 1982, ALIG mark:
　　Left: crimped as shown in catalog, 6.6" high, $75-85.
　　Right: flared (non-catalog), 6.4" high, $125+.

Figure 147. Star & File Compote, #6122, Caramel Slag (all non-catalog), IG mark:
　　Left: flared, 6.2" high, date unknown, $150+.
　　Middle: straight, 6.5" high, date unknown, $150+.
　　Right: crimped, 6.0" high, date unknown, $150+

Figure 148. Star Holly (Leaf) Covered Dish, #759 or 46876, 6.5" wide, Ruby Slag, 1971-75, satin 1971-75, IG mark, $75-85.

Figure 150. Butterpat Covered Dish, #736, 5.6" high, Caramel Slag (non-catalog), date unknown, IG mark, $600+.

Figure 149. Star Holly (Leaf) Covered Dish, #759 or 46876, 6.5" wide, Caramel Slag (non-catalog), date unknown, IG mark, $600+.

Figure 151. Rose Covered Butter Dish, #161 or 43615, 7.8" wide, Caramel Slag (non-catalog), date unknown, LIG mark, $600+.

Figure 152. 4-Toed Beaded Edge Covered Dish, #6992, 7.7" long, Purple Slag, 1971, IG mark, $400-450.

Figure 154. 2-Handled Clothes Basket Covered Dish, #456, 7.4" long, Purple Slag, 1960 (six months only), IG mark, $900+.

Figure 153. 4-Toed Beaded Edge Covered Dish, #6992, 7.7" long, Caramel Slag, 1971, IG mark, $350-400.

Figure 155. Iron (Flat) Covered Dish, #971, 8.5" long, Purple Slag, 1962-68, not marked, $225-250.

Figure 156. Heart (Leaf) Covered Dish, #312, 6.0" long, Purple Slag, 1962-67, not marked, $225-250.

Figure 157. Partitioned (Dresser) Covered Box, #191, 8.5" long, Purple Slag, 1962-68, IG mark, $225-250.

Figure 158. Beehive (Honey) Covered Jar, #60 or 43906, 5.0" high, IG mark (L. G. Wright had a very similar mold, see Figure 454 for comparison):
  Left: Purple Slag, 1974, satin 1974, $60-70.
  Middle: Jade Slag, 1975-76, satin 1975-76, $80-90.
  Right: Caramel Slag, 1964-76, satin 1973-76, $45-50.

Figure 159. Waverly Covered Dish, #1519/59, 5.2" wide, Caramel Slag, 1964-70, Heisey mold, not marked or Heisey mark, $90-100.

Figure 160. Chevron Covered Dish, #1560 or 43897, 4.6" wide, IG mark:
Left: Ruby Slag, 1972-76, satin 1972-76, $40-45.
Right: Purple Slag, 1969-74, satin 1973-74, $50-55.

Figure 161. Chevron Covered Dish, #1560 or 43897, 4.6" wide, IG mark:
Left: Jade Slag, 1975-76, satin 1975-76, $55-65.
Right: Caramel Slag, 1969-76, satin 1973-76, $35-40.

Figure 162. Lace Edge Covered Dish, #780 or 43888, 6.5" high, Purple Slag, 1962-73, satin 1973, not marked or IG mark, $65-75.

Figure 163. The Lace Edge Covered Dish, #780, had two bottom designs:
   Left: plain, not marked.
   Right: 6-loop design, IG mark.

Figure 164. Lace Edge Footed Covered Dish, #78, 9.6" high, Caramel Slag, 1964-1967, not marked, $110-120.

Figure 165. The Lace Edge Footed Covered Dish, #78, had two bottom designs, both not marked:
   Left: petal design.
   Right: plain.

Figure 166. Pokal Covered
Jar, #464 or 43910, 9.2"
high, Jade Slag, 1975,
satin 1975, not marked,
$275-300.

Figure 168. Pokal Covered
Jar, #464 or 43910, 9.2"
high, Ruby Slag, 1975,
satin 1975, not marked,
$275-300.

Figure 167. Pokal Cov-
ered Jar, #464 or 43910,
9.2" high, Purple Slag,
9.2" high, 1962-67, not
marked, $225-250.

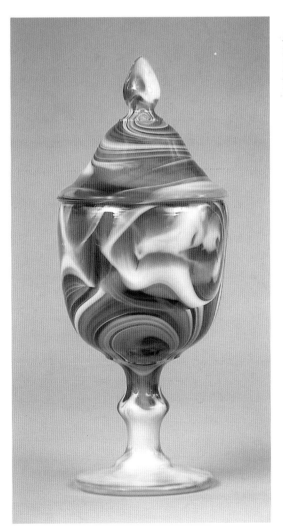

Figure 169. Pokal Covered
Jar, #464 or 43910, 9.2"
high, Caramel Slag, 1975,
satin 1975, not marked,
$175-200.

Figure 170. Chroma Footed Covered Dish, #123 or 43735, 9.5″ high, Caramel Slag, 1982, ALIG mark, $125-135.

Figure 172. Whiskbroom Footed Covered Jar, #611, 7.7″ high, Caramel Slag, 1970, IG mark, $325-375.

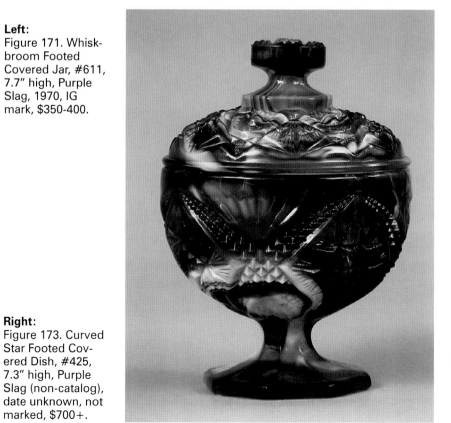

Left:
Figure 171. Whiskbroom Footed Covered Jar, #611, 7.7″ high, Purple Slag, 1970, IG mark, $350-400.

Right:
Figure 173. Curved Star Footed Covered Dish, #425, 7.3″ high, Purple Slag (non-catalog), date unknown, not marked, $700+.

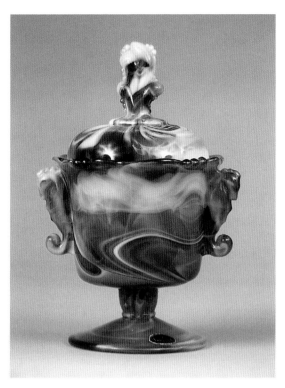

Figure 174. Seahorse (Waverly) Footed Covered Jar, #1519/140, 8.5" high, Caramel Slag, 1964-70, Heisey mold, not marked or Heisey mark, $100-120.

Figure 176. Louis (4-Toed) Covered Jar, #176 or 43882, 6.6" high:
  Left: Ruby Slag, 1969-70 & 1975, satin 1975, IG mark, $65-75.
  Right: Jade Slag, 1975, satin 1975, IG mark, $120-140.

Figure 175. Dolphin Footed Covered Jar, #2006, 7.3" high, Purple Slag, 1959-61, IG mark, $200-225.

Figure 177. Louis (4-Toed) Covered Jar, #176 or 43882, 6.6" high:
  Left: Caramel Slag, 1975, satin 1975, IG mark, $75-85.
  Right: Purple Slag, 1960-73, not marked or IG mark, satin 1973, IG mark, $75-85.

Figure 178. Saddle (Zipper) Covered Jar, #133, 7.7" high, Caramel Slag, 1964-67, IG mark, $135-165.

Figure 179.
    Left: Large Apothecary Covered Jar, #704, 9.1" high, Purple Slag, 1962-63, not marked, $425-475.
    Right: Small Apothecary Covered Jar, #702, 7.2" high, Purple Slag, 1962-63, not marked, $400-450.

Figure 180. Pie Wagon Covered Box, #377 or 43890, 6.2" long, Caramel Slag, 1982, ALIG mark, $325-375.

Figure 181. Bellaire Cruet & Stopper, Purple Slag, #505 or 43490, 1965-74, satin 1973-74:
   Left: 6.8" high, design on bottom, IG mark, $75-85
   Right: 7.0" high, smooth bottom, not marked, $75-85

Figure 182. The Bellaire Cruet & Stopper, #505, Purple Slag, mold changed in early 1970s from a smooth hand-formed bottom with large handle to pressed bottom with small handle:
   Left: pressed design, IG mark.
   Right: smooth, not marked.

Figure 183. Bellaire Cruet & Stopper, Caramel Slag, #505 or 43490, 1965-76, satin 1973-76:
   Left: 6.5" high, design on bottom, IG mark, $50-55.
   Right: 7.0" high, smooth bottom, not marked, $50-55.

Figure 184. The Bellaire Cruet & Stopper, #505, Caramel Slag, mold changed in early 1970s from a smooth hand-formed bottom with large handle to pressed bottom with small handle:
   Left: pressed design, IG mark.
   Right: smooth, not marked.

Figure 185. Bellaire Cruet & Stopper, #505 or 43490, 6.8" high:
  Left: Jade Slag, 1975-76, satin 1975-76, IG mark, $95-110.
  Right: Ruby Slag (non-catalog), date unknown, IG mark, $1000+.

Figure 186. Cask Bottle & Stopper, #1, 11.3" high, Purple Slag, 1962-63, not marked, $750-850.

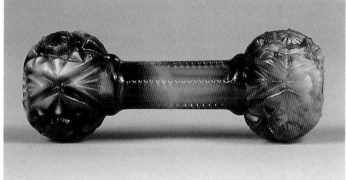

Figure 187. Carving Knife Rest, #303, 4.1" long, Ruby Slag (non-catalog), date unknown, IG mark, $600+.

Figure 188. Bird Feeder (pulley system not shown), #50, 8.5" high, Caramel Slag (non-catalog), not marked, $1800+.

Figure 189.
  Left: Grape Tumbler, #473 or 43060, 4.0" high, Ruby Slag,
  1974-75, satin 1975-75, IG mark, $25-30.
  Right: Provincial Footed Tumbler 9 oz, #1506, 4.3" high, Ruby
  Slag (non-catalog), date unknown, not marked, $375+.

Figure 191.
  Left: Eagle & Star Mug, #154 or 43329, 4.0" high, Ruby Slag,
  1971-73, satin 1971-73, IG mark, $30-35.
  Right: Eagle Wine Glass (Cigarette Holder), #1776 or 43240,
  4.0" high, Ruby Slag, 1971-75, satin 1971-75, IG mark, $25-
  30.

Figure 190
  Left: Scroll Tumbler 12 oz, #322, 5.2" high, Purple Slag, 1960
  (six months only), IG mark, $100-125.
  Right: Scroll Tumbler 10 oz, #322, 4.2" high, Purple Slag,
  1960 (six months only), IG mark, $100-125.

Figure 192. Elephant (Storybook) Mug, #1591 or 43320, 3.1"
high, Heisey mold, IG mark:
  Left: Jade Slag, 1975-76, satin 1975-76, $55-60.
  Middle: Caramel Slag, 1975-76, satin 1975-76, $35-40.
  Right: Ruby Slag, 1975-76, satin 1975-76, $45-50.

Figure 193. Robin Mug, #210 or 43325, 3.5" high, IG mark:
Left: Caramel Slag, 1970-73, satin 1973, $25-30.
Middle: Purple Slag, 1960-73, satin 1973, $35-40.
Right: Ruby Slag, 1969-75, satin 1969-75, $30-35.

Figure 195.
Left: Wine (Juice) Glass 8 oz, #552, 6.6" high, Purple Slag (non-catalog), date unknown, not marked, $375+.
Middle: Goblet 11 oz, #552, 6.7" high, Caramel Slag, 1962-63, not marked, $65-75.
Right: Wine (Juice) Glass 5.5 oz, #552, 5.8" high, Caramel Slag, 1962-63, not marked, $35-40.

Figure 194.
Left: Hoffman House Wine 6 oz, #46, 4.7" high, Jade Slag (non-catalog), c.1975, not marked, $300+.
Middle: Hoffman House Goblet 12 oz, #46, 6.3" high, Purple Slag, 1962-67, not marked, $70-80.
Right: Octagon Goblet, #593, 5.3" high, Purple Slag, 1961-68, not marked, $55-60.

Figure 196.
Left: West Virginia Commemorative "Toasting Tumbler" or Vase, 11 oz (non-catalog), #552, 5.2" high, Caramel Slag, 1963, not marked, $175+. Made as part of the West Virginia "Centennial Keepsakes" in 1963 with the state seal as a fired-on decal.
Middle: Tumbler 11 oz, #552, 5.2" high, Caramel Slag, 1962-63, not marked, $45-50.
Right: Footed Dessert (Sherbet) 5 oz, #552, 2.6"high, Caramel Slag, 1962-63, not marked, $85-95.

Figure 197.
  Left: Cape Cod Cordial (Lighter without insert), #1602, 3.6"
  high, Purple Slag (non-catalog), not marked, $40+.
  Middle: Punch Cup, #780, 3.0" high, Purple Slag, 1962-63,
  not marked, $75-85.
  Right: Panel-Sided Tumbler, mold number unknown, 3.9"
  high, Caramel Slag (non-catalog), c.1982, ALIG mark,
  $250+.

Figure 198. Windmill Pitcher 1 pint, #240 or 43150, 6.5" high:
  Left: Purple Slag, 1960-74, satin 1973-74, not marked & IG
  mark, $80-90.
  Right: Ruby Slag, 1969-76, satin 1969-76, IG mark $70-80.

Figure 200. Windmill Pitcher, #240 or 43150, 6.5" high, Purple
Slag with carnival finish (non-catalog), date unknown, IG mark,
$850+.

Figure 199. Windmill Pitcher 1 pint, #240 or 43150, 6.5" high,
IG mark:
  Left: Caramel Slag, 1964-76, satin 1973-76, $60-70.
  Right: Jade Slag, 1975-76, satin 1975-76, $100-110.

Figure 201. Miniature Pitcher (Toothpick Holder), #104 or 43636, 3.1"
high, IG mark:
   Left: Purple Slag, 1969-74, satin 1973-74, $25-30.
   Middle: Caramel Slag, 1969-75, satin 1973-75, $20-25.
   Right: Jade Slag, 1975, satin 1975, $65-75.

Figure 202. Panel-Sided Pitcher 36 oz,
#6007 or 43154, 7.7" high, Caramel Slag,
1982, ALIG mark, $100-125.

Figure 203. Olden Pitcher, #981, 5.2"
high, Purple Slag, 1962-67, not marked,
$80-90.

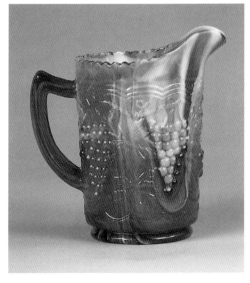

Figure 204. Grape Pitcher, #473 or 43150,
6.2" high, Caramel Slag (non-catalog),
date unknown, IG mark, $350+.

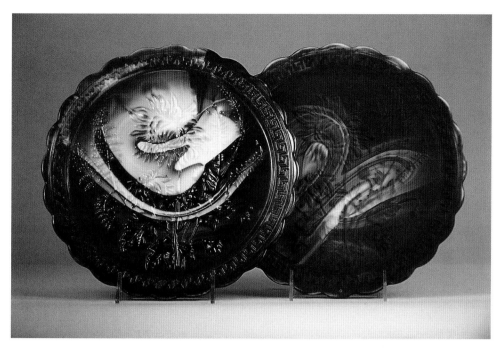

Figure 205. Mum (Chrysanthemum) Plate, #524, 10.5"
wide, Ruby Slag (non-catalog), date unknown, IG mark:
  Left: glossy, $250+.
  Right: satin, $350+.

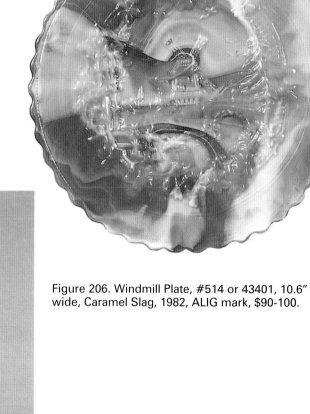

Figure 206. Windmill Plate, #514 or 43401, 10.6"
wide, Caramel Slag, 1982, ALIG mark, $90-100.

Figure 207. Rose Plate whimsey from 3-Toed
Rose Bowl (#74C), 9.6" wide, Caramel Slag
(non-catalog), date unknown, IG mark, $300+.

Figure 208. Candlewick 2-Handled Plate, #400/52D, 8.6" long, Caramel Slag (non-catalog), c.1965, not marked, $150+.

Not shown: Candlewick Plate, #400/62D, 8.5" wide, Caramel Slag (non-catalog), c.1965, not marked, $250+; Candlewick Plate, #400/42D, 5.8" wide, Caramel Slag (non-catalog), c.1965, not marked, $250+; Candlewick 2-Handled Plate, #400/145D, 13.6" long, Caramel Slag (non-catalog), c.1965, not marked, $550+.

Figure 210. Cake (Bakers) Stand, #98, 10.2" wide, Purple Slag, 1959-60, not marked, $275-325. This piece was made by joining two separate molds using molten glass on the upper part of the pedestal foot.

Figure 209. Candlewick 2-Handled Plate, crimped, #400/145C, 13.6" long, Caramel Slag (non-catalog), c.1965, not marked, $450+.

Figure 211.
   Left: Cane Salt & Pepper Set, #666 or 43487, 3.6" high, Caramel Slag, 1982, not marked, $45-50.
   Right: Caprice Salt Dip, #61 or 43657, 2.0" wide, Ruby Slag, 1971-73, satin 1971-73, IG mark, $20-25.

Figure 212. Rose Cream & Sugar Set, #588, Purple Slag, 1960-61, IG mark, $110-140 pair:
   Left: Sugar Bowl, 2.9" high.
   Right: Creamer, 3.1" high.

Figure 213. Rose Cream & Sugar Set, #588, Caramel Slag (non-catalog), date unknown, IG mark, $650+ pair:
   Left: Sugar Bowl, 2.9" high.
   Right: Creamer, 3.1" high.

Figure 214. Owl Cream & Sugar Set, #335 or 43540, Purple Slag, 1970-74, satin 1973-74, IG mark, $60-65 pair:
 Left: Sugar Bowl, 3.3" high.
 Right: Creamer, 3.5" high.

Figure 216. Owl Cream & Sugar Set, #335 or 43540, Ruby Slag, 1974-75, satin 1974-75, IG mark, $60-65 pair:
 Left: Sugar Bowl, 3.3" high.
 Right: Creamer, 3.5 high.

Figure 215. Owl Cream & Sugar Set, #335 or 43540, Jade Slag, 1975, satin 1975, IG mark, $85-95 pair:
 Left: Sugar Bowl, 3.3" high.
 Right: Creamer, 3.5" high.

Figure 217. Owl Cream & Sugar Set, #335 or 43540, Caramel Slag, 1970-75, satin 1973-75, IG mark, $45-50 pair:
 Left: Sugar Bowl, 3.3" high.
 Right: Creamer, 3.5" high.

Figure 218. Owl Cream & Sugar Set, #335, private production (non-catalog), Purple Slag, c.1965, marked SVPNT (Sears Vincent Price National Treasures) for a special promotion by Sears, Roebuck and Company, about 360 pair were made, eye color can be amber or bright orange as shown, $225+ pair:
  Left: Sugar Bowl, 3.3" high.
  Middle: Creamer, 3.5" high.
  Right: bottom showing SVPNT mark.

Figure 219. Lace Edge Cream & Sugar Set, #30, Caramel Slag, 1964-70, IG mark, $60-65:
  Left: Sugar Bowl, 3.4" high.
  Right: Creamer, 3.7" high.

Figure 220. Cane Cream & Sugar Set, #666 or 43530, Caramel Slag, 1982, ALIG mark, $65-70 pair:
  Left: Sugar Bowl, 3.7" high.
  Right: Creamer, 4.0" high.

Figure 221. Bellaire Toothpick Holder, #505 or 43624, 2.6" high, IG mark:
  Left: Caramel Slag, 1969-76, satin 1973-76, $20-25.
  Middle: Jade Slag, 1975-76, satin 1975-76, $30-35.
  Right: Purple Slag, 1969-74, satin 1973-74, $25-30.

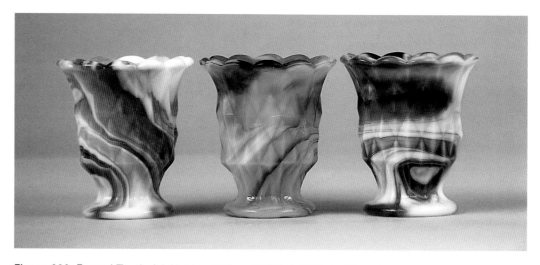

Figure 222. Footed Toothpick Holder, #19 or 43630, 2.9" high, IG mark:
  Left: Caramel Slag, 1970-75, satin 1973-75, $20-25.
  Middle: Jade Slag, 1975, satin 1975, $30-35.
  Right: Purple Slag, 1970-74, satin 1973-74, $25-30.

Figure 223. Miniature Pitcher (Toothpick Holder), #104 or 43636, 3.1" high, IG mark:
  Left: Caramel Slag, 1969-75, satin 1973-75, $20-25.
  Middle: Purple Slag, 1969-74, satin 1973-74, $25-30.
  Right: Jade Slag, 1975, satin 1975, $65-75.

Figure 224. Colonial 2-Handled Toothpick Holder, #600, 2.4" high, some may have faint Iron Cross mark:
  Left bottom: Blue Slag light, 1965-66, $50-60.
  Left top: Caramel Slag, 1965-67, $35-40.
  Middle bottom: Blue Slag dark, 1965-66, $50-60.
  Right top: Purple Slag, 1965-67, $40-45.
  Right bottom: Jade Slag, 1965-67, $45-50.

Figure 225. Cornucopia Toothpick Holder, #123 or 43528, 3.2" high, Cambridge mold:
  Left: Caramel Slag, 1974-75, satin 1974-75, IG mark, $20-25; 1982, ALIG mark, $25-30.
  Middle Left: Purple Slag, 1974, satin 1974, IG mark, $30-35.
  Middle Right: Jade Slag, 1975, satin 1975, IG mark, $35-40.
  Right: Ruby Slag, 1969-75, satin 1969-75, IG mark, $25-30.

Figure 226. Three-In-One Toothpick Holder, #1 or 43620. 2.5" high:
  Left: Ruby Slag, 1969-76, satin 1969-76, IG mark, $20-25.
  Right: Caramel Slag, 1982, ALIG mark, $25-30.

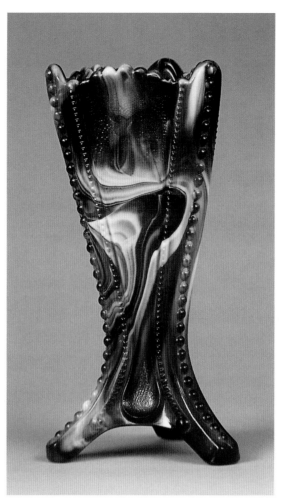

Far left:
Figure 227. Tricorn Vase, #192 or 43762, 8.5" high, Purple Slag, 1959-60, IG mark, $300-350.

Left:
Figure 228. Tricorn Vase, #192 or 43762, 8.5" high, Ruby Slag, 1975, satin 1975, IG mark, $200-225.

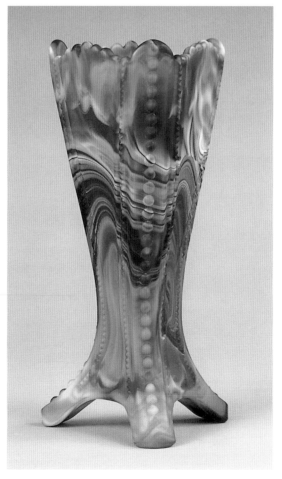

Far left:
Figure 229. Tricorn Vase, #192 or 43762, 8.5" high, Caramel Slag, 1975, satin 1975, IG mark, $200-225.

Left:
Figure 230. Tricorn Vase, #192 or 43762, 8.5" high, Jade Slag, 1975, satin 1975, IG mark, $200-225.

Left:
Figure 231. Swung Vase whimsey (non-catalog) from Tricorn Vase (#192), Ruby Slag, 12.0" high, c.1975, IG mark, $450+.

Below, left:
Figure 232. Sawtooth (Celery) Footed Vase, #194, 9.2" high, Purple Slag, 1960 (six months only), IG mark, $250-300.

Right:
Figure 233. Sawtooth (Celery) Footed Vase, #194, 9.2" high, Caramel Slag, 1964-68, not marked, $75-85.

Figure 234. Grid & Flowers Vase, #661 or 43752, 5.1" high, IG mark:
  Left: Caramel Slag, 1974-75, satin 1974-75, $50-55.
  Middle: Jade Slag, 1975, satin 1975, $75-85.
  Right: Purple Slag, 1974, satin 1974, $55-60.

Figure 235. Robin Mug Flower Arranger, #210/1, 4.0" high, same as Robin Mug mold #210, but flared for flower frog insert, IG mark:
    Left: Ruby Slag (non-catalog), date unknown, $65+.
    Right: Purple Slag, 1962-68, $60-65.

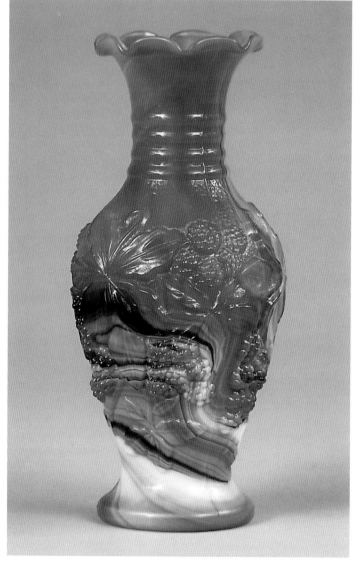

Figure 236. Panel Footed Vase, mold number unknown, 9.8" high, Ruby Slag (non-catalog), date unknown, IG mark, $400+.

Figure 237. Loganberry Vase, #109, 6.3" high, Purple Slag (non-catalog), date unknown, IG mark, $350+.

Figure 238. Nucut Footed Vase, #529 or 43770, 10.0" high, Jade Slag, 1975, satin 1975, IG mark, $250-275.

Figure 239. Nucut Footed Vase, #529 or 43770, 10.0" high, Ruby Slag, 1975, satin 1975, IG mark, $225-250.

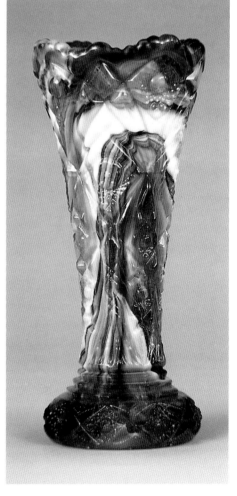

Figure 240. Nucut Footed Vase, #529 or 43770, 10.0" high, Caramel Slag, 1975, satin 1975, IG mark, $225-250.

Left:
Figure 241. Dancing Ladies (Nudes) Vase, #132 or 43638, 8.6" high, Ruby Slag, 1969-73, satin 1969-73, not marked or IG mark, $90-100.

Below, left:
Figure 242. Pinched Top Footed Vase, #965 or 43771, 9.2" high, Ruby Slag, 1969-73, satin 1969-73, not marked, $85-95.

Figure 243. Pinched Top Footed Vase (two variations), #965 or 43771, 9.5" high, Caramel Slag, 1982, ALIG mark, $110-120.

Figure 244. Pinched Top Footed Vase, #965 or 43771 had two bottom designs:
    Left: Ruby Slag, plain, not marked.
    Middle: Caramel Slag, plain, ALIG mark.
    Right: Caramel Slag, sunburst design, ALIG mark.

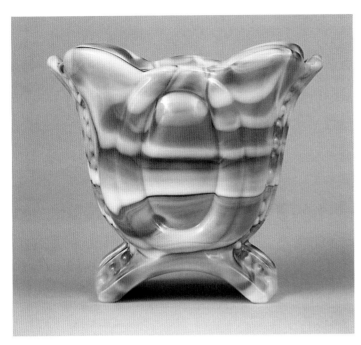

Figure 245. Saddle (Zipper) Vase, #133/1, 5.6" high, Caramel Slag, 1964-67, IG mark, same as Saddle Covered Jar (#133) without lid, $50-60.

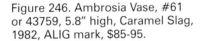

Figure 246. Ambrosia Vase, #61 or 43759, 5.8" high, Caramel Slag, 1982, ALIG mark, $85-95.

Figure 247. Cane Vase, #666 or 43763, Caramel Slag, 1982, ALIG mark:
Left: as shown in catalog, 6.4" high, $80-90.
Middle: flared (non-catalog), 6.0" high, $125+.
Right: crimped (non-catalog), 6.0" high, $125+.

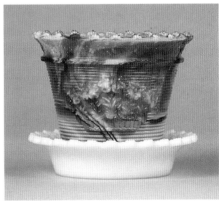

Figure 248. Flower Pot, mold number unknown, 4.1" high, Caramel Slag (non-catalog) with Milk Glass Tray, date unknown, marked MMA (Metropolitan Museum of Art), $300+ as shown with Milk Glass saucer.

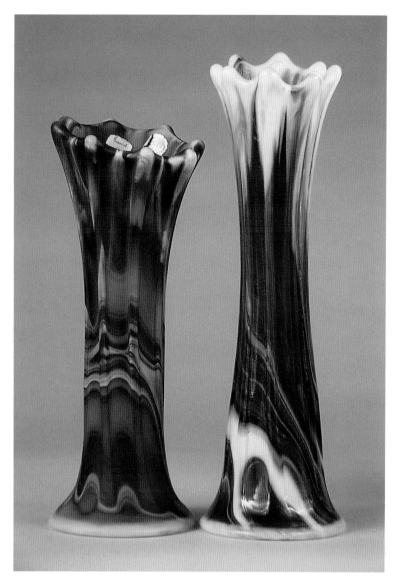

Figure 249. Swung Vase (two variations), #284, 9-13" high, Ruby Slag, 1969-70, satin 1969-70, IG mark, $100-110.

Figure 250. Small Swung Vase (two variations), mold number unknown, 5-8" high, Ruby Slag (non-catalog), not marked, $100+.

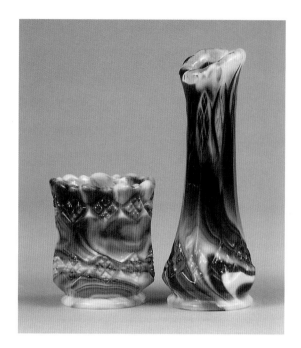

Figure 251.
Left: Three-In-One Toothpick Holder, #1 or 43620, 2.5" high, Ruby Slag, 1969-76, satin 1969-76, IG mark, $20-25.
Right: Swung Vase whimsey (non-catalog) from Three-In-One Toothpick Holder (#1), 5.0" high, Ruby Slag, date unknown, IG mark, $100+.

Figure 252.
Left: Swung Vase whimsey (non-catalog) from Owl Creamer (#335), 7.0" high, Ruby Slag, date unknown, IG mark, $100+.
Right: Owl Creamer, #335 or 43540, 3.5" high, Ruby Slag, 1974-75, satin 1974-75, IG mark, $60-65 creamer & sugar pair.

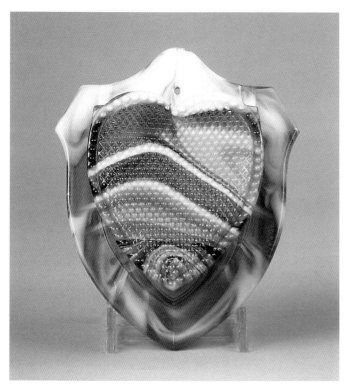

Figure 253. Heart Wall Pocket, #895, 6.0" high, Caramel Slag (non-catalog), c.1982, ALIG mark, $1000+.

Figure 255. Acorn Vase, #662 or 43765, 4.3" high, Caramel Slag (non-catalog), date unknown, IG mark, $300+.

Figure 254. Cornucopia Vase, #107, 4.7" high, Caramel Slag (non-catalog), c.1982, ALIG mark, $600+.

Figure 256. Wavy Edge Vase, mold number unknown, 5.6" high, Caramel Slag (non-catalog), c.1982. ALIG mark $350+.

Chapter 3

Westmoreland Glass Company

General History

The Westmoreland glass history began in 1889 when two brothers, Charles H. and George R. West, started the Westmoreland Specialty Company. Early products included candy and mustard containers often in clear or Opal (Milk Glass). One mold used was their version of the familiar hen-on-nest covered dish. Within a few years, they began making tableware patterns. In 1920, George R. West left Westmoreland because he was unhappy with the direction of the company. Charles H. West then become president, and James J. Brainard joined the company as treasurer. By 1925, the name had been changed to the Westmoreland Glass Company.

In these early years, many tabletop patterns and colors emerged with items often being decorated. Pieces were trimmed in gold, hand painted, and wheel engraved. One special process Westmoreland used was casing a crystal piece with colored glass dust and fusing it permanently to the surface through reheating.

After Charles H. West retired in 1937, James J. Brainard took over ownership and operation of Westmoreland. His son, James H. Brainard, had joined the company in 1933. The success of the 1920s was replaced by difficulties in the Depression era of the 1930s. Many changes were made in response to these challenging financial times including eliminating colored (except for Milk Glass) and decorated glass that had previously been at the center of the company's operation. Many pattern lines were also discontinued.[8]

Westmoreland survived these years and by the 1950s found itself in a strategic position for the growing popularity of Milk Glass. Their history with Milk Glass connects back to their earliest years. Also, considering the fact that they made some of the best Milk Glass on the market, this put them in a position to profit greatly from its popularity. Much of this ware was marketed as "Authentic Handmade Reproductions." In 1953, James J. Brainard died and his son James H. became president. Westmoreland would continue under his direction for the next 28 years.[9]

In the 1960s after the appeal of Milk Glass had started to wane, Westmoreland again made colored glass. Decorated items had been reintroduced in the 1950s when the Roses and Bows motif was painted on Milk Glass items. Decorations continued on colored glass in the 1970s and early 1980s.

In 1981, James H. Brainard sold the company to David Grossman who introduced new colors and revived old molds; however, his efforts were ultimately in vain and the company closed in early 1984.[10]

Slag and Marble Names

In all of Westmoreland's catalogs the name Marble was used; however, all of the pieces made for private productions, such as for the Levay Distributing Company or Jennings Red Barn, were sold under the name of Slag. In the photo captions, we will use the name Marble for items sold by Westmoreland and Slag for all others.

Marble History at Westmoreland

Westmoreland's first Marble catalog items appeared in 1972 when both Purple Marble and Green Marble were introduced. Overall, Purple Marble had the longer duration and was made for five years. The Green Marble was discontinued after three years. Many of the molds used, in either color, were only in a catalog for one or two years before being discontinued and replaced by another. With Green Marble, at least three distinct shades of green can be found: a light pastel or mint green, a pea green, and an olive shade. The 1973 catalog shows the Cat Covered Dish on a Rectangular Lacy base and is unique in that the cat top is in Purple Marble and the base in Milk Glass. When Green Marble was discontinued in 1975, it was replaced by Brown Marble, which was produced through 1976. The 1977-78 catalog had no Marble colors available.

The next color was in the 1979 catalog and was made for that one year only. Oddly enough, it was never given an official name; instead, the catalog simply calls it "Marble." Because it is a mixture of Milk Glass and a color Westmoreland called Almond, we have used the name Almond Marble. However, some collectors have also used the name Caramel Marble or Caramel Marble Light. Westmoreland's last color was a single item in yet another unnamed Marble color in the 1982 catalog. The 5" Cat Covered Dish on the Split Rib base was shown in Ruby Marble. It was the only Ruby Marble item made for any catalog. Westmoreland's chemist, Dwight Johnson, would have been responsible for developing all these Marble colors. As with Axel Otto-son at Imperial, Dwight Johnson deserves much credit for his success with Westmoreland's Marble colors.

In 1982, Westmoreland produced a number of non-catalog Marble items in Blue Marble and in variations of red and orange colors. Any item in the Blue Marble is very difficult to find. The Raised Wing Swan, as shown in Figure 289, is one example. The story is often told that only seven of the Rectangular Lacy bases were successfully produced.

For the red, orange, and yellow variations, collectors have usually used Ruby Marble as a collective name for the red and dark orange colors, and Butterscotch Marble for the light yellow-orange color. Considering the difficulty of making Ruby Marble and the general inconsistency of the color, the red-orange-yellow variations are not surprising. It is difficult to say if the Butterscotch Marble is an unsuccessful version of red or if it was intentional. When comparing the Fox Covered Dish made for Levay in Figure 303 with the one in Figure 304, it is logical that, at least in this situation, the orange-yellow version is a variation due to the difficult nature and inconsistency of the color. As mentioned earlier, the Cat Covered Dish is the only Ruby Marble piece found in any catalog. In that piece, the red color sometimes becomes brown as shown in Figure 299.

Mold Numbers

The numbering system used by Westmoreland centered on "Line" numbers to designate various patterns. For instance, the Paneled Grape pattern was called Line #1881 and the Old Quilt pattern was Line #500. Individual molds did not have numbers. For collectors, it was sometimes a challenge to identify one mold from another. When organizing her first book on Westmoreland, Lorraine Kovar decided to resolve this problem by assigning many of Westmoreland's popular molds and patterns with individual mold numbers. Each Line or pattern was given a two letter abbreviation followed by numbers for individual molds. For all photo captions, both the Kovar and Line number will be given whenever possible.

Mold Marks and Factory Stickers

On all Westmoreland-made Marble items, if an item were marked, only the "WG" mold mark was used. It consists of the two letters overlapped. See Figure 257 for an example. During the last few years before closing, David Grossman introduced the final mold mark where the name "Westmoreland" was written in a circle around an abstracted "W." We have never seen a Marble item made by Westmoreland with this mark.

When an item is found with its original sticker, it will consist of "Westmoreland Glass" in a circle around the words "Authentic Handmade." Also, some items will still

Figure 257. Example of "WG" logo mark on many Westmoreland pieces.

have their original ware sticker with their name in black at the top usually followed by the Line number, item description, and suggested retail price as shown in Figure 293. Westmoreland did not use hangtags with their Marble items.

Private Productions

Of primary importance in documenting the Marble production of Westmoreland are the items made for the L. G. Wright Glass Company and for the Levay Distributing Company. Both of these companies used the name Slag instead of Marble. For L. G. Wright, Westmoreland made many of the Purple and Ruby Slag, all of the Caramel Slag, and possibly some of the Blue Slag items. That will be discussed more in Chapter 4.

The histories of Westmoreland, Fenton, and Imperial all overlap with Levay, which operated by both the names of Levay Distributing Company and Levay Glass Company. Owned by Gary and Dodie Levi and located in Edwardsville, Illinois, Levay contracted with various glass factories to make limited edition pieces for them. Sometimes individual items were made, but much more frequently collections of ten to twenty pieces would be made using mold and color combinations that were new to the market. Gary particularly liked Carnival items and also reviving old molds and patterns, such as Westmoreland's High Hob pattern (Line #550), that had gone unused for many years. Fenton, Imperial, and the L. E. Smith Glass Company all made special pieces for Levay. At one point, Levay also produced a studio art glass line at their Edwardsville location.

It is clear from our conversations with Gary & Dodie Levi that their relationship with Westmoreland was a rather special one. Westmoreland made the first pieces for them in 1973 and continued to do so until Westmoreland closed in 1984. Gary Levi spent a fair amount of time at the Westmoreland factory and developed a close relationship with many of the people there. His energy and creativity was no doubt infectious. He reports that there were many discussions about colors, molds, and items for possible production. Wonderful pieces were made for Levay. Not surprisingly, many were Carnival. Today, because all of these items were limited editions, Westmoreland enthusiasts know that finding some items can often be difficult. It seems fair to say that in a great many ways, Westmoreland and Levay benefited each other.

For our concerns, Westmoreland made two significant Slag colors for Levay. The first was Purple Slag Carnival made in 1977-78. Often, the same pieces were made for Levay without the Carnival finish. Pieces without the Carnival finish were not exclusive to Levay. In previous years, some of these Slag items had been in various Westmoreland catalogs. The Purple Slag Carnival collection included animal covered dishes, pitcher and tumbler sets, a cookie jar, and several butter dishes. Some pieces were signed Levay, dated and numbered, but many were not. See Figure 392 for an example of a signed piece and Figures 258 and 259 for copies of a Levay advertising flyer and an invoice from Westmoreland to Levay. Some Levay advertising gives quantities of how many were made of a particular item. Keep in mind that these quantities were approximations.

The second important color was Ruby Slag produced in 1982, the same year that Westmoreland made Ruby Slag for L. G. Wright (they called it Red Slag). For reasons probably relating to production problems, very few of these pieces were made. As already mentioned in Chapter 1, some of these items may be found with cracks in them. If a piece is rare, a crack might be acceptable in order to acquire it for your collection. To our knowledge, none of these Ruby Slag pieces (some are more orange in color) were listed in any Levay advertising brochures and Gary Levi recalls that most were probably sold by word of mouth to his regular customers. Because it is difficult to know which exact items were made for Levay and which are feasibility or test items, the photo captions use the name Ruby Marble for consistency. It is also possible that at least some of these Ruby Marble animal dishes were originally sold on Milk Glass bases, at least they are frequently found that way today. Apparently, more Ruby Marble animal tops were successfully made than bases. Also, many of these large animal covered dishes in any color can be found with the original eyes still intact.

For the record, Levay is still in operation today and continues to have glass made in many wonderful colors. Their connection to Westmoreland continues in that Levay owns several Westmoreland molds including animal covered dishes such as the Raised Wing Swan (RSW-1), Fox (FX-1), Eagle (#EA-1), Large Rooster (#RO-2), Rabbit with Eggs (#RB-4), Rectangular Cat (#CT-1), and Lamb (#LB-2).

A smaller but important group of animal covered dishes were also made for Jennings Red Barn in New Martinsville, West Virginia. In 1982, Westmoreland produced the 5" size swan, hen, rooster, lamb, and rabbit in "Iridescent" Butterscotch Slag although the color is typically called Butterscotch Slag Carnival. See Figure 260 for a copy of one of their advertisements. Although not in a Carnival finish, Westmoreland also made this color in 1982 for L. G. Wright. They called it Caramel Slag.

The last private production items of interest to us are a group made for the A.A. Importing Company from St. Louis. In 1975, Westmoreland made six pieces of Purple Slag for them. See Figure 261 for a copy of a catalog page from that year. Three were in a Westmoreland catalog at one point or another (cat, duck and owl) in Purple Marble, and the other three (rabbit, lamb, and plate) were probably made exclusively for A.A. Importing.

Items Not Shown

We have documented some items that have not been photographed. You will see a text box describing them.

Often, these pieces are quite rare and we simply were not able to photograph them. However, all such items have either been documented in a catalog or we have personally seen the piece.

Reproductions and Imports

Westmoreland has had the "honor" of having more molds being reproduced or copied than any of the other three companies in this book. Some companies that purchased molds after Westmoreland closed have sometimes produced pieces without removing the Westmoreland mold marks. Fortunately, all original Marble items from Westmoreland carry the older WG mark. If a Slag item is found with the later Westmoreland Circle mark, it is not original to Westmoreland. Some molds that were never made in any Slag color by Westmoreland show up in Slag bearing a WG mark such as the Santa on Sleigh (#1872-1) in Red Slag as shown in Figure 566. If you see a Westmoreland item in Slag, and it is not documented in this book, assume that it is not original Westmoreland, especially if it has the Westmoreland Circle mark.

Taiwan imports have included items from both original Westmoreland molds and copied versions. The Three Kittens 7" Plate (#KP-1) and Chick on Oval Two-handled Basket (#CK-1) are at least two items from Taiwan that we know have been made in Purple Slag from original Westmoreland molds and carry a WG mark. Other molds have been copied such as the Oval Duck Covered Dish (#OD-1) and Standing Rooster Covered Dish (#SR-1). The mold quality on the import pieces is often poor. Figure 295 compares the heads of a Westmoreland Oval Duck and its Taiwan counterpart. Figure 279 compares the two Standing Rooster molds. In the past, the quality of glass from import items such as these was also very poor, but in recent years the quality has greatly improved. Some of their Purple Slag looks surprising like what has been made by American factories. We expect the mold quality will also soon be noticeably better.

Values

Westmoreland items deserve a special note about values. Compared to the current prices of Imperial and Fenton pieces in particular, we are surprised that values for Westmoreland Marble are not generally higher. We know from experience that there are fewer collectors for Westmoreland Marble than for Imperial or Fenton Slag. However, considering the high quality of molds, colors, and overall scarcity, we do not really understand why. Rare Westmoreland items will frequently sell for half of the typical price for an Imperial or Fenton item of equal scarcity! If the collector base for Westmoreland Marble expands, the values quoted in this book will likely soon be outdated.

Figure 258. Copy of an advertising page from the Levay Distributing Company (Levay Glass Company) showing items in Purple Slag and Purple Slag Carnival, dated 1977.

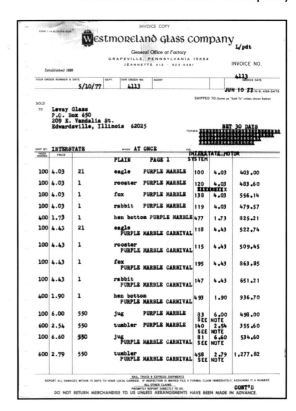

Figure 259. Copy of invoice from Westmoreland to the Levay Distributing Company (Levay Glass Company) dated June 10, 1977, showing items in Purple Marble and Purple Marble Carnival.

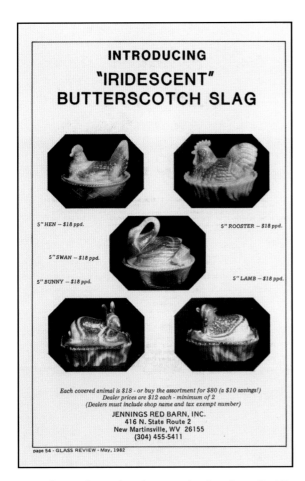

Figure 260. Copy of an advertisement by Jennings Red Barn showing the five Butterscotch Slag Carnival animal covered dishes from the *Glass Review*, May, 1982, p. 54, Vol. 12, No. 4.

Figure 261. Copy of a page from the 1975 catalog from A.A. Importing Company show Purple Slag items made for them by Westmoreland.

Figure 262. Hen Covered Dish (Diamond Basketweave base), #HN-2 (#2), 5.5" long:
  Left: Brown Marble (non-catalog), c.1975, WG mark, $250+.
  Right: Butterscotch Slag Carnival, private production (non-catalog) for Jennings Red Barn,
    1982, WG mark, $85+.

Figure 263. Hen Covered Dish (Diamond Basketweave base), #HN-2 (#2), 5.5" long:
  Left: Purple Marble, 1978, WG mark, $75-85.
  Right: Purple Slag Carnival, private production (non-catalog) for Levay Distributing Co.,
    1978, WG mark, $150+.

Figure 264. Hen Covered Dish (Diamond Basketweave base), #HN-2 (#2), 5.5" long,
Ruby Marble (non-catalog), c1982, WG mark, $100+.

Figure 265. Large Hen Covered Dish (Diamond Basketweave base), #HN-1 (#1), 7.4" long, Purple Marble, 1972 & 1978, WG mark, $275-325.

Figure 267. Large Hen Covered Dish (Smooth Rim base), #HN-1 (#1), 7.1" long, Purple Marble (non-catalog), date unknown, WG mark, $325+.

Figure 266. Large Hen Covered Dish (Diamond Basketweave base), #HN-1 (#1), 7.4" long, Purple Slag Carnival, private production (non-catalog) for Levay Distributing Co., 1978, WG mark, $375+.

Figure 268. Large Hen Covered Dish (Diamond Basketweave base), #HN-1 (#1), 7.4" long, Green Marble, (Diamond Basketweave base), 1972-73, WG mark, $85-110.

Figure 269. Large Hen Covered Dish (Diamond Basketweave base), #HN-1 (#1), 7.4" long, Ruby Marble, private production (non-catalog) for Levay Distributing Co., 1982, WG mark, $450+.

Not shown: Large Hen Covered Dish (Diamond Basketweave base), #HN-1 (#1), 7.4" long, Blue Marble (non-catalog), c.1982, $500+.

Figure 270. Large Hen Covered Dish (Diamond Basketweave base), #HN-1 (#1), 7.4" long, Butterscotch Marble (non-catalog), c.1982, WG mark, $300+.

Figure 271. Chick Covered Dish (two examples), #CK-2 (#3), 2.5" long, Ruby Marble (non-catalog), c.1982, WG mark, $125+.

Figure 272. Large Rooster Covered Dish (Diamond Basketweave base), #RO-2 (#1), 7.4" long, Butterscotch Marble (non-catalog), c.1982, WG mark, $300+.

Figure 274. Large Rooster Covered Dish (Diamond Basketweave base), #RO-2 (#1), 7.4" long, Purple Marble, 1972 & 1977, WG mark, $275-325.

Figure 273. Large Rooster Covered Dish (Diamond Basketweave base), #RO-2 (#1), 7.4" long, Purple Slag Carnival, private production (non-catalog) for Levay Distributing Co., 1977, WG mark, $375+.

Figure 275. Large Rooster Covered Dish (Diamond Basketweave base), #RO-2 (#1), 7.4" long, Ruby Marble, private production (non-catalog) for Levay Distributing Co., 1982, WG mark, $450+.

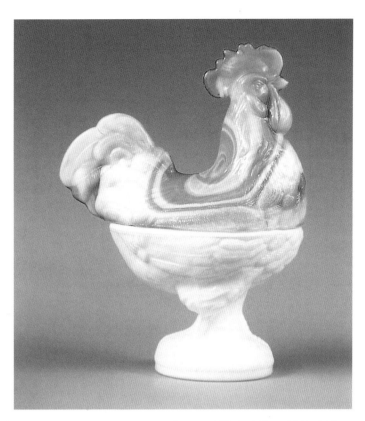

Figure 276. Standing Rooster Covered Dish, #SR-1 (#6), 8.6" high, Butterscotch Marble (non-catalog), c.1982, WG mark, $300+ for matched top and base. Shown with a Milk Glass base but can be found with Butterscotch Marble base.

Figure 278. Standing Rooster Covered Dish, #SR-1 (#6), 8.6" high, Purple Marble, 1972, WG mark, $175-200.

Not shown: Standing Rooster Covered Dish, #SR-1 (#6), 8.6" high, WG mark: Blue Marble (non-catalog), c.1982, $400+; and Ruby Marble (non-catalog), c.1982, $400+.

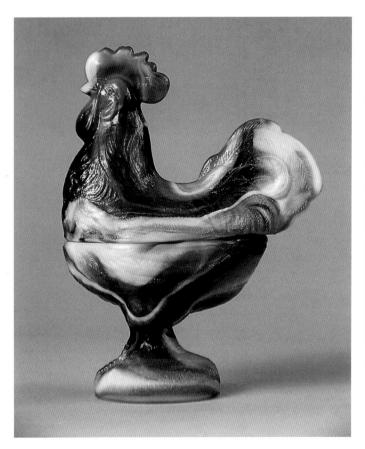

Figure 277. Standing Rooster Covered Dish, #SR-1 (#6), 8.6" high, Brown Marble (non-catalog), c.1975, WG mark, $300+.

Figure 279.
   Left: Taiwan Import Standing Rooster Covered Dish, 8.5" high, Purple Slag, not marked, base is textured down to bottom edge.
   Right: Westmoreland Standing Rooster Covered Dish, 8.6" high, Purple Marble, WG mark, base has .25" smooth band around the bottom edge of base.

Figure 280. Rooster Covered Dish (Vertical Rib base), #RO-3 (#2), 5.5" long, WG mark:
  Left: Butterscotch Slag Carnival, private production (non-catalog) for Jennings Red Barn, 1982, $85+.
  Right: Purple Marble, 1978, $75-85.

Not shown: Rooster Covered Dish (Vertical Rib base), #RO-3 (#2), 5.5" long, Purple Slag Carnival, private production (non-catalog) for Levay Distributing Glass Co., 1978, WG mark, $150+.

Figure 282. Robin on Twig Nest, #RB-1 (#7), 5.8" high, Almond Marble, 1979, WG mark, $110-135.

Figure 281. Robin on Twig Nest, #RB-1 (#7), 5.8" high, Purple Marble, 1972, WG mark, $325-375.

Figure 283. Robin on Twig Nest, #RB-1 (#7), 5.8" high, Ruby-Orange Marble (non-catalog), c.1982, WG mark, $300+ for matched top and base. Shown with a Milk Glass base but can be found with Ruby-Orange Marble base.

Figure 284. Love Birds Covered Dish, #LB-1 (#20), 5.9" long, Purple Marble, 1972, WG mark, $125-150.

Figure 286. Love Birds Covered Dish, #LB-1 (#20), 5.9" long, Ruby-Orange Marble (non-catalog), c.1982, WG mark, $250+.

Figure 285. Love Birds Covered Dish, #LB-1 (#20), 5.9" long, Brown Marble, 1975-76, WG mark, $90-100.

Figure 287. Love Birds Covered Dish, #LB-1 (#20), 5.9" long, Almond Marble, 1979, WG mark, $75-85.

Figure 290. Raised Wing Swan Covered Dish (Rectangular Lacy base), #RWS-1 (#1873), 9.6" long, Purple Marble, 1975-76, WG mark, $425-475.

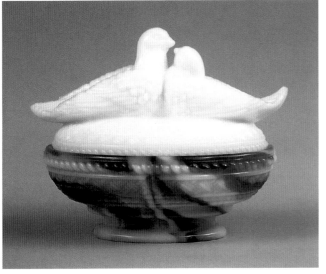

Figure 288. Love Birds Covered Dish, #LB-1 (#20), 5.9" long, Blue Marble base with Milk Glass top (non-catalog), c.1982, WG mark, $150+ as shown. Unknown if Blue Marble top was made.

Figure 291. Swan Covered Dish (Diamond Basketweave base), #SW-4, 5.5" long, Butterscotch Slag Carnival, private production (non-catalog) for Jennings Red Barn, 1982, WG mark, $85+.

Figure 289. Raised Wing Swan Covered Dish (Rectangular Lacy base), #RWS-1 (#1873), 9.6" long, Blue Marble (non-catalog), c.1982, WG mark, $1000+.

Not shown: Swan Covered Dish (Diamond Basketweave base), #SW-4, 5.5" long, Blue Marble (non-catalog), c.1982, WG mark, $250+.

Figure 292. Oval Duck Covered Dish, #OD-1 (#10), 7.9" long, Almond Marble, 1979, WG mark, $110-135.

Figure 294. Oval Duck Covered Dish, #OD-1 (#10), 7.9" long, Purple Marble, 1975-76 & 1978, WG mark, $125-150 (Also made as a private production for A. A. Importing Co., 1975).

Figure 293. Oval Duck Covered Dish, #OD-1 (#10), 7.9" long, Purple Slag Carnival, private production (non-catalog) for Levay Distributing Co., 1978, WG mark, $250+.

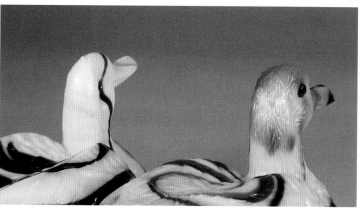

Figure 295.
  Left: Taiwan Import Oval Duck Covered Dish, Purple Slag, not marked, head is .5" thick and smooth, poor mold quality.
  Right: Westmoreland Oval Duck Covered Dish, #OD-10 (#10), WG mark, head is .75" thick and textured.

Not shown: Oval Duck Covered Dish, #OD-1 (#10), 7.9" long, Blue Marble (non-catalog), c.1982, WG mark, $400+.

Figure 296. Cat Covered Dish (Rectangular Lacy base), #CT-1 (#1/1870), 8.1" long, Almond Marble, 1979, WG mark, $325-375.

Figure 297. Cat Covered Dish (Rectangular Lacy base), #CT-1 (#1/1870), 8.1" long, Green Marble, 1972, WG mark, $325-375.

Figure 298. Cat Covered Dish (Rectangular Lacy base), #CT-1 (#1/1870), 8.1" long, Purple Marble top with Milk Glass base as shown in catalog, 1973, WG mark, $250-300. Can be found with Purple Marble base (non-catalog), $400+.

Figure 299. Cat Covered Dish (Vertical Rib base), #CT-2 (#18), 5.5" long, WG mark:
  Left: Ruby Marble (with brown variation), 1982, $70-80.
  Right: Ruby Marble, 1982, $70-80.

Figure 300. Cat Covered Dish (Vertical Rib base), #CT-2 (#18), 5.5" long, WG mark:
  Left: Purple Slag Carnival, private production (non-catalog) for Levay Distributing
    Co., 1978, WG mark, $125+.
  Right: Purple Marble, 1972-73, 1975-76, & 1978, $65-75 (Also made as a private
    production for A. A. Importing Co., 1975).

Figure 301. Lion Covered Dish (Diamond Basketweave base), #LI-1 (#1), 7.4" long,
Purple Marble, 1973, WG mark, $250-300.

Figure 302. Fox Covered Dish (Diamond Basketweave base), #FX-1 (#1), 7.4" long, Purple Marble, 1972 & 1977, WG mark, $275-325.

Figure 303. Fox Covered Dish (Diamond Basketweave base), #FX-1 (#1), 7.4" long, Ruby Marble, private production (non-catalog) for Levay Distributing Co., 1982, WG mark, $450+.

Figure 304. Fox Covered Dish (Diamond Basketweave base), #FX-1 (#1), 7.4" long, Orange Marble (non-catalog), c.1982, WG mark, $400+.

Not shown: Fox Covered Dish (Diamond Basketweave base), #FX-1 (#1), 7.4" long, Purple Slag Carnival, private production (non-catalog) for Levay Distributing Co., 1977, WG mark, $375+.

Figure 305. Lamb Covered Dish (Picket Fence base), #LB-2, 5.4" long:
  Left: Butterscotch Slag Carnival, private production (non-catalog) for Jennings Red Barn, 1982, WG mark, $85+.
  Right: Purple Slag, private production (non-catalog) for A. A. Importing Co., 1975 $75+.

Figure 306. Eagle Covered Dish (Diamond Basketweave base), #EA- 1 (#21), 7.4" long, Purple Marble, 1977, WG mark, $250-300.

Figure 308. Eagle Covered Dish (Smooth Rim base), #EA- 1 (#21), 7.1" long, Ruby Marble, private production (non-catalog) for Levay Distributing Co., 1982, WG mark, $400+.

Not shown: Eagle Covered Dish (Diamond Basketweave base), #EA- 1 (#21), 7.4" long, Purple Slag Carnival, private production (non-catalog) for Levay Distributing Co., 1977, WG mark, $375+.

Figure 309. Mule Eared Rabbit (Picket Fence base), #RB-3 (#5), 5.4" long, WG mark:
Left: Butterscotch Slag Carnival, private production (non-catalog) for Jennings Red Barn, 1982, $85+.
Right: Purple Slag, private production (non-catalog) for A. A. Importing Co., 1975, $75+.

Figure 307. Eagle Covered Dish (Diamond Basketweave base), back view, #EA- 1 (#21), 7.4" long, Purple Marble, 1977, WG mark, $250-300.

Figure 310. Rabbit with Eggs Covered Dish, (Diamond Basketweave base), #RB-4 (#1), 7.4" long, Purple Marble, 1977, WG mark, $200-225.

Figure 311. Rabbit with Eggs Covered Dish (Diamond Basketweave base), #RB- 1 (#1), 7.4" long, Purple Slag Carnival, private production (non-catalog) for Levay Distributing Co., 1977, WG mark, $375+.

Figure 312. Rabbit with Eggs Covered Dish (Diamond Basketweave base), #RB-4 (#1), 7.4" long, Ruby Marble, private production (non-catalog) for Levay Distributing Co., 1982, WG mark, $400+.

Figure 313. Rabbit with Eggs Covered Dish, #RB-4 (#1), 7.8" long, Purple Marble on Milk Glass Lacy base (non-catalog), 1977, WG mark, $175+ as shown.

Not shown: Some large animal tops can be found with Purple Marble Lacy base (non-catalog), 7.8" long, WG mark. $450+ for any animal on a Purple Marble Lacy base.

Figure 314. Wren (Milk Glass square base), #WR-2 (#5), 3.5"
wide, WG mark on base:
  Left: Green Marble (non-catalog), c.1973, $65+; without base,
    not marked, $50+.
  Right: Purple Marble (non-catalog), c.1973, $65+; without base,
    not marked, $50+.

Figure 316. Owl on Tree Stump (1 Pound Owl), #OS-1
(#1), 5.5" high, not marked:
  Left: Almond Marble, 1979, $35-40.
  Right: Purple Marble (non-catalog), date unknown,
    $40+.

Figure 315. Owl on Books, OOB-1 (#10), 3.5" high, WG mark:
  Left: Purple Marble, 1975-76, $25-30 (Also made as a private
    production for A. A. Importing Co., 1975).
  Middle Left: Brown Marble Carnival (non-catalog), c.1975,
    $40+.
  Middle Right: Brown Marble, 1975-76, $30-35.
  Right: Almond Marble (non-catalog), c.1979, $30+.

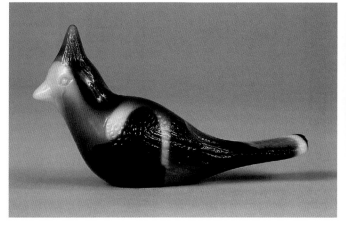

Figure 317. Cardinal, #CD-1 (#11), 5.1" long, Purple
Marble, 1972, WG mark, $55-65.

Figure 318.
Left: Large Butterfly, #BF-1 (#3), 4.6" wide, Brown Marble on Milk Glass square base (non-catalog), 1975-76, WG mark, $50+.
Middle Left: Large Butterfly, #BF-1 (#3), 4.6" wide, Green Marble, 1972, not marked, $45-50.
Middle: Small Butterfly, #BF-2 (#2), 2.4" wide, Purple Marble (non-catalog), c.1972, not marked, $50+.
Middle Right: Large Butterfly, #BF-1 (#3), 4.6" wide, Purple Marble on Milk Glass square base (non-catalog), c.1975, WG mark, $50+.
Right: Large Butterfly, #BF-2 (#2), 4.6" wide, Brown Marble Carnival (non-catalog), c.1975, WG mark, $50+.

Not shown: Small Butterfly, #BF-2 (#2), 2.4" wide, Green Marble (non-catalog), not marked, $50+.

Figure 320. Owl Toothpick Holder, #OT-1, Line #62, 2.9" high, WG mark:
Left: Brown Marble, 1975-76, $25-30.
Middle: Green Marble, 1972, $25-30.
Right: Purple Marble, 1972, $25-30.

Figure 319. Rocky Horse, private production (non-catalog) for Guernsey Glass Co., 4.4" long, Ruby Slag, their color name was Carousel Slag, 1981, "Rocky" & 1981 mark, $35+.

Figure 321. Swan Toothpick Holder, #SW-2, Line #115, 2.3" high, Purple Marble, 1974, WG mark, $30-35.

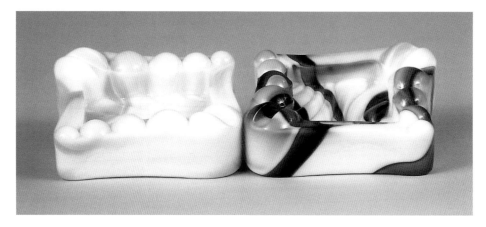

Figure 322. Swirl & Ball Ashtray, #SB-41, Line #1842, 3.4" wide, not marked:
  Left: Green Marble, 1973, $25-30.
  Right: Purple Marble, 1973, $25-30.

Figure 323. Bird Ashtray (Pipe Holder), #BA-1, Line #10, 5.1" long, not marked:
  Top: Purple Marble (non-catalog), c.1972, $55+.
  Bottom: Green Marble (non-catalog), c.1972, $50+.

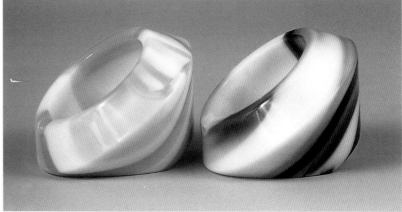

Figure 325. Slanted Round Ashtray, #1972-1, Line #1972, 3.4" wide, not marked:
  Left: Green Marble, 1972-73, $25-30.
  Right: Purple Marble, 1972-73, $25-30.

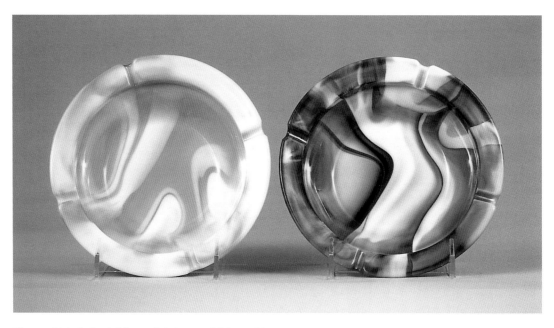

Figure 324. Colonial Round Ashtray, #CO-11, Line #1776, 7" wide, not marked:
  Left: Green Marble, 1972-74, $30-35.
  Right: Purple Marble, 1972-74, $35-40.

Figure 326. Pansy Split-Handled Basket, #PB-1, Line #757, 4.7" wide, WG mark:
  Left: Green Marble, 1972-73, $50-55.
  Right: Purple Marble, 1972-73, $55-65.

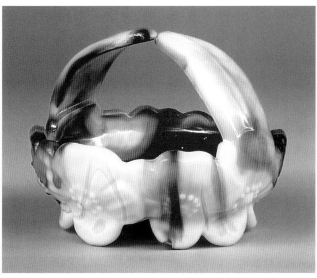

Figure 327. Pansy Split-Handled Basket, #PB-1, Line #757, 4.7" wide, Ruby Marble (non-catalog), c.1982, WG mark, $200+.

Figure 328. Small Basket, #BK-1, Line #750, 6.5" wide, WG mark:
  Left: Purple Marble, 1975-76, $55-65.
  Right: Brown Marble, 1975-76, $50-55.

Figure 329. English Hobnail Basket, #EH-73, Line #555, 8.9" high, Ruby Marble, private production (non-catalog) for Levay Distributing Co., 1982, WG mark, $450+.

Figure 330. Paneled Grape Split-Handled Oval Basket, #PG-86, Line #1881, 6.5" long, Brown Marble, 1975-76, WG mark, $55-65.

Figure 331. Paneled Grape Split-Handled Oval Basket, #PG-86, Line #1881, 6.5" long, Purple Marble, 1974-76, WG mark, $65-75.

Figure 332. Paneled Grape Split-Handled Oval Basket, #PG-86, Line #1881, 6.5" long, Green Marble, 1974, WG mark, $100-125.

Figure 333. Woolworth Scallop Rim Grape Basket, #WW-7, Line #89, 5.7" wide, Purple Marble (non-catalog), date unknown, not marked, $300+.

Figure 334. Smooth Bowl, crimped & ruffled, #1900-6, Line #1900, 8.2" wide, Orange Marble (non-catalog), c.1982, not marked, $125+.

Figure 335. Smooth Bowl, crimped & ruffled, #1900-6, Line #1900, 8.2" wide, Green Marble, 1972-73, not marked, $40-50.

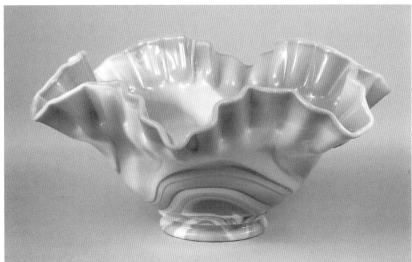

Figure 336. Smooth Bowl, crimped & ruffled, #1900-6, Line 1900, 8.2" wide, Purple Marble, 1974-76, not marked, $75-85.

Figure 337. Paneled Grape Dish, crimped & ruffled, #PG-15, Line #1881, 8" wide, Brown Marble (non-catalog), c.1975, WG mark, $100+.

Figure 338. Star Centerpiece Bowl, #300-1, Line #300, 11.5" wide, Purple Marble, 1972-76, not marked or WG mark, $55-65.

Figure 340. Star Centerpiece Bowl, #300-1, Line #300, 11.5" wide, Brown Marble, 1975-76, WG mark, $55-65.

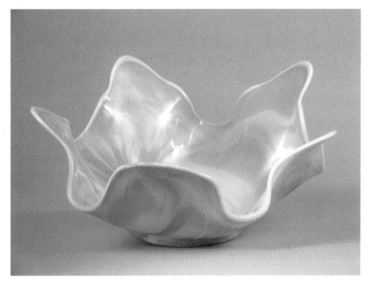

Figure 339. Star Centerpiece Bowl, #300-1, Line #300, 11.5" wide, Green Marble, 1972-74, not marked or WG mark, $45-55.

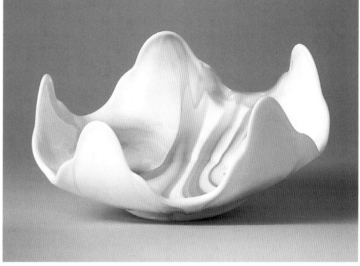

Figure 341. Star Centerpiece Bowl, #300-1, Line #300, 11.5" wide, Orange Marble (non-catalog), c.1982, WG mark, $125+.

Figure 342. Doric Oval Bowl, #DO-19, Line #3, 12.7" long, Brown Marble, 1975-76, WG mark, $70-80.

Figure 344. Doric Oval Bowl, #DO-19, Line #3, 12.7" long, Green Marble, 1974, WG mark, $100-125.

Not shown: Doric Oval Bowl, #DO-19, Line #3, 12.7" long, WG mark: Ruby Marble (non-catalog), c.1982, $300+; and Blue Marble (non-catalog), c.1982, $400+.

Figure 343. Doric Oval Bowl, #DO-19, Line #3, 12.7" long, Purple Marble, 1974-76, WG mark, $85-95.

Figure 345. 3-Footed Nut Dish, satin finish, #1914-1, Line #1914, 4.9" wide, Light Blue Marble (non-catalog), date unknown, not marked, $100+.

Figure 346. Three Ball Bowl, cupped rim, #1067-1, Line #1067, 10.5" wide, Green Marble, 1972, not marked, $150-175.

Figure 347. Three Ball Bowl, cupped rim, #1067-1, Line #1067, 10.5" wide, Purple Marble, 1972, not marked, $175-200.

Figure 348. Three Ball Bowl, flared rim, #1067-1, Line #1067, 12.8" wide, Purple Marble (non-catalog), c.1972, not marked, $200+.

Figure 349. Small bowl, ground foot, mold number unknown, 5.3" wide, Purple Marble (non-catalog), not marked, $125+. Assumed to be Westmoreland because it was purchased at their factory outlet store.

Figure 350. Rose & Lattice Bowl, crimped & ruffled, #RL-11, Line # 1967, 8.2" wide, Purple Marble (non-catalog), date unknown, WG mark, $150+.

Figure 351. Rose & Lattice Bowl, cupped & crimped, #RL-11, Line #1967, 6.0" wide, Purple Marble (non-catalog), date unknown, WG mark, $150+.

Figure 352. "Bulb" bowl, cupped & crimped, mold number unknown, 5.6" wide, Purple Marble (non-catalog), date unknown, WG mark, $150+.

Figure 353. Smooth low bowl whimsey, mold number unknown, 8.0" wide, Purple Marble (non-catalog), not marked, $75+. Assumed to be Westmoreland because it was purchased near the factory.

Figure 354. Footed Candleholder with satin finish shade, #CL-1, Line #1972, 7.7" high, not marked:
   Left: Purple Marble, 1974, $75-85.
   Right: Green Marble, 1974, $65-75.

Figure 356. Spiral Candleholder, #SP-1, Line #1933, 6.3" high, WG mark:
   Left: Purple Marble, 1972-76, $85-95 pair.
   Middle: Green Marble, 1972-74, $75-85 pair.
   Right: Brown Marble, 1975-76, $80-90 pair.

Not shown: Spiral Candleholder, #SP-1, Line #1933, 6.3" high, Ruby Marble (non-catalog), c.1982, WG mark, $250+ pair.

Figure 355. Three Ball Candleholders, satin finish, #TE-21, Line #1067, 2.8" high, Purple Marble (non-catalog), date unknown, not marked, $200+ pair.

Figure 357. Paneled Grape Candleholder, #PG-20, Line #1881, 4.0" high, Orange Marble (non-catalog), c.1982, WG mark, $250+ pair.

Figure 358. Paneled Grape Compote, #PG-114, Line #1881, 4.1" high, Purple Marble, 1974-76, WG mark, $65-75.

Figure 359. Paneled Grape Compote, #PG-114, Line #1881, 4.1" high, Brown Marble, 1975-76, WG mark, $55-65.

Figure 360. Paneled Grape Compote, #PG-114, Line #1881, 4.1" high, Green Marble, 1974, WG mark, $55-65.

Figure 361. Lotus Compote, crimped, #LO-19, Line #1921, 3.6" high, Green Marble, 1972, WG mark, $40-45.

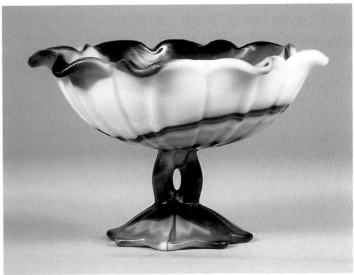

Figure 362. Lotus Compote, crimped, #LO-19, Line #1921, 3.6" high, Purple Marble, 1972, WG mark, $45-50.

Figure 363. Colonial 2-Handled Sweetmeat Compote, #CO-16, Line #1776, 5.9" high, Green Marble, 1972-74, WG mark, $55-65.

Figure 365. Colonial 2-Handled Sweetmeat Compote, #CO-16, Line #1776, 5.9" high, Orange Marble (non-catalog), c.1982, WG mark, $125+.

Figure 364. Colonial 2-Handled Sweetmeat Compote, #CO-16, Line #1776, 5.9" high, Brown Marble, 1975-76, WG mark, $55-65.

Figure 366. Colonial 2-Handled Sweetmeat Compote, #CO-16, Line #1776, 5.9" high, Purple Marble, 1972-76, WG mark, $65-75.

Figure 367. Ashburton Compote, crimped, #AB-15, Line #1855, 4.7" high, WG mark:
   Left: Green Marble, 1974, $50-55.
   Right: Purple Marble, 1974, $55-65.

Figure 368. Ashburton Compote, crimped, #AB-15, Line #1855, 4.3" high, Brown (Caramel) Marble (non-catalog), date unknown, WG mark, $125+.

Figure 369. Doric Sweetmeat Compote, crimped, #DO-34, Line #3, 5.1" high, WG mark:
   Left: Brown Marble, 1975-76, $50-55.
   Right: Purple Marble, 1975-76, $55-65.

Figure 370. Compote, #1902-2 without lid, Line #1902, 5.5" high, Brown Marble (non-catalog), c.1975, WG mark, $100+.

Figure 371. Thousand Eye Covered Dish, #TE-22, Line #1000, 4.5" wide, WG mark:
  Left: Green Marble, 1974, $65-75.
  Right: Purple Marble, 1974, $75-85.

Figure 373. Sawtooth Covered Dish, #ST-2, Line #556, 6.5" wide, Purple Marble, 1973-74, WG mark, $85-95.

Figure 372. Paneled Grape Covered Dish, #PG-34, Line #1881, 4.6" wide, WG mark:
  Left: Green Marble, 1974, $75-85.
  Right: Purple Marble, 1974, $85-95.

Figure 374. Sawtooth Covered Dish, #ST-2, Line #556, 6.5" wide, Green Marble, 1973-74, WG mark, $75-85.

Figure 375. Octagon Footed Covered Dish, #1211-1,
Line #1211, 8.0" high, WG mark:
    Left: Green Marble, 1974, $65-75.
    Right: Purple Marble, 1974, $75-85.

Figure 376. Swirl & Ball Covered Dish, #SB-16, Line
#1842, 7.2" high, WG mark:
    Left: Green Marble, 1973, $65-75.
    Right: Purple Marble, 1973, $75-85.

Figure 377. Cherry (Thumbprint) Footed Covered
Dish, #CH-12, Line #109, 5.6" wide, WG mark:
    Left: Green Marble, 1972, $75-85.
    Right: Purple Marble, 1972, $85-95.

Figure 378. Cherry (Thumbprint) Footed Covered
Dish, #CH-12, Line #109, 5.6" wide, Orange Marble
(non-catalog), c.1982, WG mark, $175+.

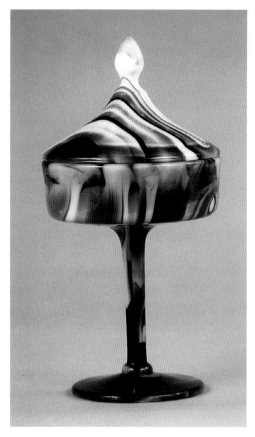

Figure 379. Sweetmeat Footed Covered Dish, #1708-13, Line #1708, 8.6" high, Purple Marble (non-catalog), date unknown, not marked, $175+.

Figure 380.
    Left: Paneled Grape Medium Canister, shown without lid, #PG –96b, Line #1881, 9.5" high approx., Purple Marble (non-catalog), 1972, WG mark, with Marble lid $650+.
    Middle: Paneled Grape Large Canister, shown with Milk Glass lid, #PG-96a, Line #1881, 10.9" high, Purple Marble, 1972, WG mark, with Marble lid $450-500.
    Right: Paneled Grape Small Canister, #PG-96c, Line #1881, 7.2" high, Purple Marble, 1972, WG mark, $200-250.

Figure 381.
    Left: Paneled Grape Large Canister, #PG-96a, Line #1881, 10.9" high, Green Marble, 1972, WG mark, $350-400.
    Right: Paneled Grape Small Canister, #PG-96c, Line #1881, 7.2" high, Green Marble, 1972, WG mark, $150-175.

Not shown: Paneled Grape Medium Canister, #PG –96b, Line #1881, 9.5" high approx., Green Marble, 1972, WG mark, $500-550.

Figure 382. Argonaut Shell Covered Dish, #AS-1, Line #1048, 6.5" high, Purple Marble, 1973-76, WG mark, $85-95.

Figure 384. Argonaut Shell Covered Dish, #AS-1, Line #1048, 6.5" high, Green Marble, 1975-76, WG mark, $75-85.

Figure 383. Argonaut Shell Covered Dish, #AS-1, Line #1048, 6.5" high, Brown Marble, 1973-74, WG mark, $75-85.

Figure 385. Cherry & Cable Cookie (Cracker) 2-Handled Covered Jar, #CH-9, Line #109, 7.7" high, Purple Marble (non-catalog), 1978, WG mark, $350+.

Not shown: Cherry & Cable Cookie (Cracker) 2-Handled Covered Jar, both colors were private production (non-catalog) for Levay Distributing Co., #CH-9, Line #109, 7.7" high, WG mark: Purple Slag Carnival, 1978, $400+; and Ruby Marble, 1982, $500+.

Figure 386. Old Quilt (Checkerboard) Butter (Cheese) Covered Dish, #OQ-11, Line #500, 7.2" wide, Purple Marble (non-catalog), 1978, WG mark, $150+.

Figure 388. Paneled Grape Butter (Cheese) Covered Dish, #PG-36, Line #1881, 7.1" wide, Purple Marble (non-catalog), 1978, WG mark, $150+.

Figure 387. Old Quilt (Checkerboard) Butter (Cheese) Covered Dish, OQ-11, Line #500, 7.2" wide, Purple Slag Carnival, private production (non-catalog) for Levay Distributing Co., 1978, WG mark, $200+.

Figure 389. Paneled Grape Butter (Cheese) Covered Dish, #PG-36, Line #1881, 7.1" wide, Purple Slag Carnival, private production (non-catalog) for Levay Distributing Co., 1978, WG mark, $200+.

Figure 390. High Hob Butter (Cheese) Covered Dish, #HH-6, Line #550, 7.4" wide, Purple Marble (non-catalog), 1978, WG mark, $150+.

Figure 393. Della Robbia Goblet 8 oz, #DR-3, Line #1058, 5.9" high, Caramel Marble (non-catalog), date unknown, WG mark, $75+.

Figure 391. High Hob Butter (Cheese) Covered Dish, #HH-6, Line #550, 7.4" wide, Purple Slag Carnival, private production (non-catalog) for Levay Distributing Co., 1978, WG mark, $200+.

Figure 392. High Hob Butter (Cheese) Covered Dish, detail of signed piece on inside of base, #HH-6, Line #550, Purple Slag Carnival, private production (non-catalog) for Levay Distributing Co. Not all Levay pieces are signed.

Figure 394. Tumbler, #PL-1, Line #1902, 3.7" high, Ruby Marble (non-catalog), c.1982, WG mark, $75+.

Figure 395. High Hob Footed Pitcher, #HH-3, Line #550, 7.8" high, Purple Marble (non-catalog), 1977, not marked, $150+.

Figure 397.
Left: Old Quilt (Checkerboard) Tumbler, #OQ-9, Line #500, 4.6" high, Purple Marble (non-catalog), 1978, WG mark, $25+.
Right: Old Quilt (Checkerboard) Pitcher, #OQ-10, Line #500, 8.4" high, Purple Marble (non-catalog), 1978, WG mark, $150+.

Not shown: High Hob Tumbler, #HH-2, Line #550, 4.0" high, Purple Marble (non-catalog), 1977, not marked, $25+. Old Quilt (Checkerboard) Tumbler, #OQ-9, Line #500, 4.6" high, Purple Slag Carnival, private production (non-catalog) for Levay Distributing Co., 1978, WG mark, $25+; and Old Quilt (Checkerboard) Pitcher, #OQ-10, Line #500, 8.4" high, Purple Slag Carnival, private production (non-catalog) for Levay Distributing Co., 1978, WG mark, $175+.

Figure 396.
Left: High Hob Tumbler, #HH-2, Line #550, 4.0" high, Purple Slag Carnival, private production (non-catalog) for Levay Distributing Co., 1977, not marked, $25+.
Right: High Hob Footed Pitcher, #HH-3, Line #550, 7.8" high, Purple Slag Carnival, Private production (non-catalog) for Levay Distributing Co., 1977, not marked, $175+.

Figure 398. Colonial Pitcher, #CO-6, Line #1776, 7.8" high, Ruby Marble (non-catalog), c.1982, not marked, $450+.

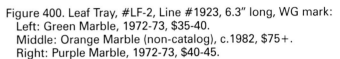
Figure 400. Leaf Tray, #LF-2, Line #1923, 6.3" long, WG mark:
  Left: Green Marble, 1972-73, $35-40.
  Middle: Orange Marble (non-catalog), c.1982, $75+.
  Right: Purple Marble, 1972-73, $40-45.

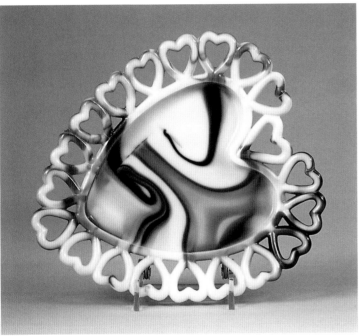

Figure 399. Heart Plate, #HP-1, Line #32, 8.0" long, Purple Slag, private production (non-catalog) for A. A. Importing Co., 1975, WG mark, $60-70.

Figure 401. Spade Coaster (Ashtray), #SP-2, Line #1820, 5.3" long, Green Marble (non-catalog), c.1973, not marked, $35+.

Figure 402. Double Hands Tray, #DH-1, Line #51, 7.5" long, Ruby Marble (non-catalog), c.1982, WG mark, $150+.

Figure 403. Paneled Grape Footed Vase, #PG-37, Line #1881, 5.5-5.8" high, WG mark:
   Left: Brown Marble, 1975-76, $45-55.
   Middle: Light Blue Marble (non-catalog), date unknown, $125+.
   Right: Purple Marble, 1975-76, $55-65.

Not shown: Paneled Grape Footed Vase, #PG-9, Line #1881, 11.5" high, Purple Marble (non-catalog), date unknown, mark unknown, $250+. Shown on cover of *Glass Review*, July/August, 1983, Vol. 13, No. 6.

Figure 405. Swirl & Ball Footed Vase, #SB-1, Line #1842, 9.1" high, Green Marble, 1973-74, WG mark, $65-75.

Figure 404. Swirl & Ball Footed Vase, #SB-1, Line #1842, 9.1" high, Purple Marble, 1973-74, WG mark, $75-85.

Figure 406. Bud Vase, #BV-2, Line #1902, 10-11" high, WG mark:
   Left: Purple Marble, 1972-76, $40-45.
   Middle Left: Ruby Marble (non-catalog), c.1982, $75+.
   Middle Right: Brown Marble, 1975-76, $35-40.
   Right: Green Marble, 1972-74, $35-40.

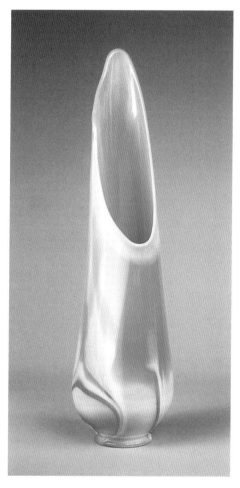

Figure 407. Smooth Vase, #1900-4, Line #1900, 15-16" high, Green Marble, 1972-73, not marked & WG mark, $55-65.

Figure 408. Smooth Vase, #1900-4, Line #1900, 15-16" high, Purple Marble, 1972-73, not marked & WG mark, $65-75.

Figure 409. Smooth Vase, flared, #1900-4, Line #1900, 11.4" high, Purple Marble (non-catalog), c.1972, not marked, $75+.

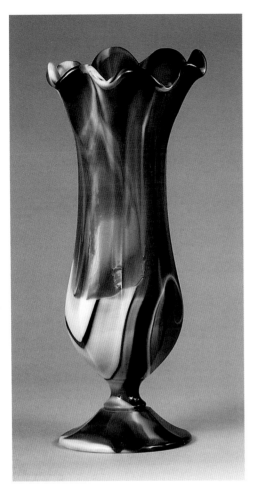

Figure 410. Colonial Footed Vase, #CO-15, Line #1776, 13-14" high, Purple Marble, 1974-76, WG mark, $75-85.

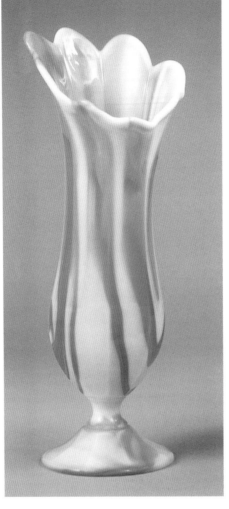

Figure 411. Colonial Footed Vase, #CO-15, Line #1776, 13-14" high, Green Marble, 1974, WG mark, $65-75.

Figure 412. Colonial Footed Vase, #CO-15, Line #1776, 13-14" high, Brown Marble, 1975-76, WG mark, $65-75.

Figure 413. Oval paperweight, mold number unknown, 5.0" long, Caramel Marble (non-catalog), date unknown, not marked, $50+.

Chapter 4

L. G. Wright Glass Company

General History

Of the four major companies represented in this book, the L. G. Wright Glass Company is the only one that was not a glass factory. However, Wright did own most of the molds that were used. Located in New Martinsville, West Virginia, L. G. Wright functioned exclusively as a glassware wholesaler. Over the years, many glass factories were involved to one degree or another in making L. G. Wight items.

Lawrence Gale Wright started his company in the mid-1930s after a short stint as a sales representative for several glass and pottery companies including the New Martinsville Glass Manufacturing Company. During that period, he met many glass & pottery manufacturers, wholesalers, and buyers and soon realized that he wanted to set up his own business. In 1938, he married Verna Mae Haught who would become an integral part of the business.

By the late 1930s, Mr. Wright had glass factories such as Fenton making items for him in colors including Cranberry and Vaseline. At the same time, he also started having his own molds made (and many more would follow) as well as buying existing molds from defunct factories such as the Dugan Glass Company and Diamond Glass-ware Company. Some of these molds, including the Cherry pattern (also called Wreathed Cherry), were later made in Slag colors.

His customers included other wholesalers, department stores, and antique dealers. Interestingly enough, one of Wright's long time customers was A.A. Sales Company from St. Louis, which in 1975 had Purple Slag made for them by Westmoreland. At that point, their name was A.A. Importing Company.

It was during these years that the first books on antique American glassware were being published and the popularity of antique glass was growing. Mr. Wright's vision to sell reproductions of this type of glassware would prove to be successful for many decades. There is no doubt that some dealers sold his new glass as antique. In department and furniture stores, Wright glassware was marketed as "Early American Style." Regardless of how it was labeled, Wright understood that beautiful glass at the right price would sell, and it did.

In the years to follow, a multitude of colors and decorations would be available in molds that replicated vintage pieces. Lamps, blown glass, pressed patterns, and ceramic items were all part of the Wright catalogs. Pressed patterns included Daisy and But-

ton, Eye-Winker, and Moon and Star. Wright's Panel Grape pattern included over fifty different molds. Many blown pitchers, cruets, and lamps were sold in Cranberry and Cranberry Opalescent. Many items were decorated, particularly lamps, and in 1968, Mr. Wright established his own decorating department. His participation in the company that bore his name, and in which he had worked so hard, ended suddenly upon his death in 1969.

Verna Mae Wright, who had previously managed the office and bookkeeping, in many ways continued where her husband had left off. New colors such as Custard were continued, Carnival Glass was introduced, more Thistle pattern molds were made, and new lamps were painted. She effectively ran the company for the next twenty years until her death in 1990. Dorothy Stephan, Mrs. Wright's cousin, and her daughter, Phyllis Stephan Buettner, continued the operation until 1999 when the L. G. Wright Glass Company was closed.[11]

Slag History at L. G. Wright

Records supplied to us by James Measell at Fenton indicate that in the early 1950s, the Lattice Edge plate and the Daisy and Button Bootie (Fenton's mold) were made for Wright in Purple Slag. Other Purple Slag pieces Wright had made in the 1950s were the Atterbury Duck Covered Dish and Large Hen Covered Dish although it is uncertain who produced them. The Daisy & Cube Goblet may also have been made during this period. Please note that this was before Imperial first made its Purple Slag items. In a 1992 interview with Lucile Kennedy, who had worked at Imperial for many years, she recalled that "there were some people making a little bit of Slag, but most of it was going to the antique dealers as reproductions."[12] She was very likely referring to these Purple Slag pieces by Wright. The Lace edge plates sold by Wright in Purple Slag are virtually indistinguishable from those made in the 1880s. Mr. Wright had the Atterbury Duck mold made in 1941. In 1948, the Large Hen Covered Dish mold was made. Having them "reproduced" in the Victorian era color of Purple Slag was good business from Mr. Wright's point of view. Both the Atterbury Duck and the Large Hen were in the Wright line in Purple Slag for nearly forty years proving beyond doubt their popularity.

In the 1960s, many other Wright items were made in Purple Slag probably either by Imperial or Westmoreland. L. G. Wright records are incomplete on this point. Considering how much Purple Slag was being made by Imperial in the 1960s, and that Westmoreland did not produce Slag for themselves until 1972, Imperial remains the better candidate. We do know that much of the Purple Slag made for Wright in the 1970s was by Westmoreland, and that Imperial made the Ruby Slag (Cherry pattern) that was introduced in 1978. In 1982, Westmoreland made both the Red Slag and Caramel Slag. Wright used both Ruby and Red names; however, for consistency in the photo captions, we will use the name Ruby. The Plum Glass Company made at least some of the Blue Slag that appeared in 1984. Mosser Glass of Cambridge, Ohio, made many of the later Slag colors. At some point, Slag animal covered dishes by Wright were offered in either the standard glossy finish or in a satin finish for a small up-charge.

Mold Marks & Mold Numbers

Few L. G. Wright items were marked. See Figure 414 for an example of their mold mark consisting of an underlined "W" in a small circle. The only Slag items with this mark are some of the Cherry pattern pieces. All mold numbers in the photo captions are the same as those used by Wright in its catalogs.

Figure. 414. Example of the "W" (underlined) in Circle mark used on a few of the L. G. Wright pieces.

Documentation of Years

Unlike other glass factories, L. G. Wright did not issue new catalogs every year. Their first published catalog dates back to 1968 and it was updated with supplements rather than printing a whole new catalog. Once a piece was made, it would often be in the line as long as supplies lasted. If it were a good seller, more would be ordered. For this reason, determining exact dates of when an item was available is often difficult compared to charting a color and mold from year to year catalogs. With L. G. Wright items, years provided in the photo captions should be understood to be approximations. For example, if the years listed are 1979-95, please do not assume that the item was available throughout all of that period. Rather, assume it was probably available for most of that period.

With the L. G. Wright Glass Company, we go beyond the titled years of this book because of the extended years that they sold Slag items. In the early 1990s, a few Slag pieces that had been made years before, could still be purchased at the factory. Sometimes, if the Slag bottoms for animal dishes were sold out, a Slag animal top would be sold with a Milk Glass base. For an example, see Figure 427.

Reproductions and Imports

When Wright closed in 1999, several molds were purchased by companies that are now using them for glass production in Taiwan. Two examples are the Cherry Pitcher and Tumbler set and the Pump and Trough set. To date, none of these molds have been found in a Slag color. As for American-made examples of glass using molds previously owned by Wright, see Chapter 6.

Values

Because so many of the L. G. Wright pieces are unmarked, much of their production is sold without the knowledge of its background. The Slag items are no exception. It can also be a little confusing to understand that Wright was a wholesale company only and not a factory. Many Slag collectors are surprised to find out that Imperial and Westmoreland made most of their Slag colors. Nonetheless, the quality of molds and Slag colors usually speak for themselves and values have increased steadily over the years.

Purple Slag was in the Wright catalogs for many more years than any of their other Slag colors. Because of this, Purple Slag is not always valued as highly, contrary to what is usually the case with other companies. Slag pieces in Caramel and Ruby can often be the most difficult to find and can garner higher prices than the same piece in Purple. Notice that the Wright pieces we could not locate to photograph for this book are mostly in Caramel Slag.

Figure 415. Small Hen Covered Dish, #70-18, 4.0" long, Purple Slag, 1966, not marked, $35-45.

Figure 416. Hen Covered Dish, #80-7, 5.4" long, not marked:
   Left: Purple Slag, 1960s, 1979-1995, $50-60.
   Middle: Blue Slag, 1984-95, $40-50.
   Right: Caramel Slag, 1982-87, $75-85.

Figure 417. Hen Covered Dish, #80-7, 5.4" long, Ruby Slag, two variations, 1982-87, not marked, $90-110.

Figure 418. Rooster Covered Dish, #80-12, 5.4" long, not marked:
   Left: Blue Slag, 1984-95, $40-50.
   Middle: Purple Slag, 1960s, 1979-95, $50-60.
   Right: Ruby (orange) Slag, 1982-87, $90-110.

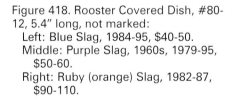

Not shown: Rooster Covered Dish, #80-12, 5.4" long, Caramel Slag, 1982, not marked, $75-85.

Figure 419. Large Hen Covered Dish, #70-8, 7.1" long, Purple Slag, 1950-60s, 1975, & 1982-1995, not marked, $75-85.

Figure 421. Large Hen Covered Dish, #70-8, 7.1" long, Caramel Slag, 1982-87, not marked, $80-100.

Figure 420. Large Hen Covered Dish, #70-8, 7.1" long, Blue Slag, 1984-95, not marked, $65-75.

Figure 422. Large Hen Covered Dish, #70-8, 7.1" long, Ruby Slag, 1982, not marked, $145-165.

Figure 423. Large Hen Covered Dish, #70-8, 7.1" long, Ruby (orange) Slag, 1982, not marked, $125-145.

Figure 424. Turkey Covered Dish, #80-15, 5.4" long, not marked:
  Left Top: Purple Slag, 1966, 1979-95, $45-55.
  Left Bottom: Caramel Slag, 1982-87, $65-75.
  Right Top: Ruby Slag, 1982, $80-100.
  Right Bottom: Blue Slag, 1984-95, $40-50.

Figure 425. Large Standing Turkey Covered Dish, #70-17, 7.6" high, Purple Slag, private production (non-catalog) for Jennings Red Barn, 50 made, 1978, not marked, $500+. Shown in advertisement from Glass Review, November 1978, p. 60, Vol. 8, No. 11.

Figure 426. Owl Covered Dish, #80-10, 5.4" long, not marked:
  Left: Caramel Slag, 1982-87, $75-85.
  Middle: Blue Slag, 1984-95, $40-50.
  Right: Purple Slag, 1966 & 1979-95, $45-55.

Figure 427. Owl Covered Dish, #80-10, 5.4" long, not marked:
  Left: Ruby Slag, 1982-87, $75-85.
  Right: Ruby Slag (orange) on Milk Glass base as sold from company outlet store, 1990s, $35-45.

Figure 428. Cow Covered Dish, #80-3, 5.4" long, not marked:
Left Top: Purple Slag, 1960s & 1979-95, $45-55.
Left Bottom: Ruby Slag, 1982-90, $75-85.
Right Top: Caramel Slag, 1982-87, $65-75.
Right Bottom: Blue Slag, 1984-95, $40-50.

Figure 429. Bull (Ferdinand) Covered Dish, #77-46, 4.3" high, not marked:
Left: Purple Slag, 1960s & 1979-84, $35-45.
Right: Caramel Slag, 1982-84, $45-55.

Figure 430. Horse Covered Dish, #80-8, 5.4" long, not marked:
Left: Ruby Slag, 1982-87, $80-100.
Right: Purple Slag, 1960s & 1979-95, $50-60.

Not shown: Horse Covered Dish, #80-8, 5.4" long, not marked: Caramel Slag, 1982-87, $75-85; Blue Slag, 1984-95, $50-60.

Figure 431. Lamb Covered Dish, #80-9, 5.4" long, not marked:
   Left: Purple Slag, 1960s & 1979-95, $45-55.
   Right: Caramel Slag, 1982-90, $55-65.

Figure 432. Cat Covered Dish, #80-2, 5.4" long, not marked:
   Left: Purple Slag, 1960s, 1979-95, $45-55.
   Middle: Caramel Slag, 1982, $55-65.
   Right: Blue Slag, 1984-95, $40-50.

Figure 433.
   Left: L. G. Wright Cat Covered Dish top, #80-2, not marked, cat sitting on textured surface.
   Right: Westmoreland Cat Covered Dish top, #CT-2. (#18), WG mark, cat sitting on smooth surface.

Figure 434. Dog Covered Dish, #80-4, 5.4" long, Purple Slag, 1960s, not marked, $75-85.

Figure 435. Atterbury Duck Covered Dish, #70-2, 10.9" long, Blue Slag, 1984-95, not marked, $60-70.

Figure 436. Atterbury Duck Covered Dish, #70-2, 10.9" long, Caramel Slag, 1982-87, not marked, $75-85.

Figure 437. Atterbury Duck Covered Dish, #70-2, 10.9" long, Purple Slag, 1950-60s, 1975-95, not marked, $75-85.

Figure 438. Duck Covered Dish, #80-5, 6.4" long, Purple Slag, 1966, not marked, $85-95.

Figure 439. Bird (Robin) Covered Dish, #80-1, 5.4" long, Purple Slag, 1966, not marked, $75-85.

Figure 442. Large Frog Covered Dish, #77-127, 8.4" long, Blue Slag, 1984-87, not marked, $75-95.

Figure 440. Swan Covered Dish, #80-14, 5.4" long, not marked:
   Left: Caramel Slag, 1982-90, $45-55.
   Right: Purple Slag, 1966 & 1979-95, $45-55.

Figure 441. Frog Covered Dish, #80-6, 5.4" long, Purple Slag, 1966, not marked, $75-85.

Figure 443. Rabbit Covered Dish, #80-11, 6.5" long, Purple Slag, 1966, not marked, $75-85.

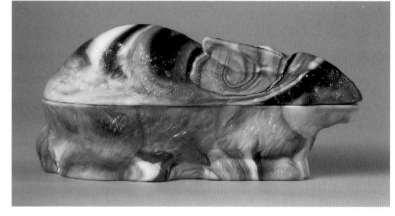

Figure 445. Atterbury Rabbit Covered Dish, #77-128, 9.5" long, Blue Slag, 1984-87, not marked, $80-100.

Figure 444.
   Top: Taiwan Import Rabbit Covered Dish, Purple Slag, 6.8" long, not marked, rear legs protrude from body.
   Bottom: L. G. Wright Rabbit Covered Dish, #80-11, 6.5" long, not marked, rear legs flush with body.

Figure 446. Turtle Covered Dish, #80-16, 5.4" long, not marked:
   Left: Purple Slag, 1960s & 1979-95, $45-55.
   Middle: Ruby (orange) Slag, 1982-90, $80-100.
   Right: Caramel Slag, 1982-90, $65-75.

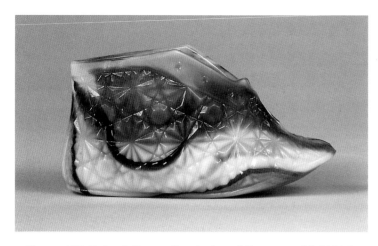

Figure 447. Daisy & Button Bootie, (used Fenton mold #1994), 4.2" long, Purple Slag, c.1953, not marked, $45-55.

Figure 449. Fish Toothpick Holder (Salt Dip), #77-59, 4.7" long, Purple Slag, 1966, not marked, $40-45.

Figure 448.
   Left: Cherry Toothpick Holder, #7-8, 2.5" high, Ruby Slag, 1978, W (underlined) in Circle mark, $25-30.
   Middle: Cherry Toothpick Holder, #7-8, 2.5" high, Purple Slag, date unknown, not marked, $25-30.
   Right: "S" Repeat Toothpick Holder, #77-63, 2.3" high, Purple Slag, 1966, not marked, $20-25.

Figure 450. Daisy & Button Fan Toothpick Holder (Vase), #22-77, 3.8" high, Purple Slag, 1966, not marked, $65-75.

Figure 451.
  Left: Large Cherry Oval Bowl, #7-16, 10.9" long, Purple Slag, 1978, not marked, $125-150.
  Right: Small Cherry Oval Bowl, #7-17, 5.0" long, Purple Slag, 1978, not marked, $35-45.

Figure 452. Cherry Scroll Compote, #7-3, 6.5" wide, Purple Slag, 1966, not marked, $55-65.

Not shown: Dolphin Compote, #72-3, 5.7" high, Purple Slag (non-catalog), date unknown, $250+. Shown in *The L. G. Wright Glass Company* by James Measell & W. C. "Red" Roetteis, p.113.

Figure 453. Beehive (Honey) Covered Jar, #77-8, 4.9" high, Purple Slag, 1966, not marked, $55-65.

Figure 454. L. G. Wright and Imperial had very similar Beehive Covered Jar molds:
  Left: Imperial lid, inside view, #60 or 43906, no flange on lid where it sits on base, bottom stippled, IG mark.
  Right: L. G. Wright lid, inside view, #77-8, flange on lid to hold it in place, bottom smooth, not marked.

Figure 455. Cherry Butter Covered Dish, #7-2, 7.7" wide, Purple Slag, 1977 & 1984, not marked, $90-100.

Figure 456. Cherry Butter Covered Dish, #7-2, 7.7" wide, Ruby Slag, c.1978, W (underlined) in Circle mark, $90-100.

Figure 457. Cherry Butter Covered Dish, #7-2, 7.7" wide, Caramel Slag, 1982, W (underlined) in Circle mark, $125-150.

Figure 458. Cherry Cream & Sugar Set, Ruby Slag, 1978, not marked, $75-85 pair:
   Left: Creamer, #7-4, 4.8" high.
   Right: Sugar Bowl, #7-5, 3.8" high.

Figure 460. Cherry Sugar Bowl, #7-5, 3.8" high, Caramel Slag, 1982, not marked, $75-85 pair.

Figure 459. Cherry Cream & Sugar Set, Purple Slag, 1966 & 1977-84, not marked, $80-90 pair:
   Left: Sugar Bowl, #7-5, 3.8" high.
   Right: Creamer, #7-4, 4.8" high.

Not shown: Cherry Creamer, #7-4, 4.8" high, Caramel Slag, 1982, not marked.

Figure 461. Pump & Trough, $125-150 set.
   Left: Trough, #77-96, 5.0" long, Purple Slag, 1977-82, not marked.
   Right: Pump, #77-95, 6.3" high, Purple Slag, 1977-82, not marked.

Figure 462. Cherry Pitcher, #7-14, 8.0" high, Ruby Slag, 1978, W (underlined) in Circle mark, $125-150.

Not shown: Cherry Pitcher, #7-14, 8.0" high, Caramel Slag, 1982, W (underlined) in Circle mark, $125-150.

Figure 464.
Left: God & Home Tumbler, #1776-T, 4.3" high, Blue Slag, 1984-95, W (underlined) in Circle mark, $15-20.
Right: God & Home Pitcher, #1776-P, 8.8" high, Blue Slag, 1984-95, W (underlined) in Circle mark, $75-85.

Figure 463. Cherry Pitcher, #7-14, 8.0" high, Purple Slag, 1977-84, W (underlined) in Circle mark, $100-125.

Figure 465. Cherry Ice Tea Glass, #7-15, 5.5" high, not marked:
  Left: Purple Slag, 1977 & 1984, $30-35.
  Middle: Caramel Slag, 1982, $30-35.
  Right: Ruby Slag, c.1978, $30-35.

Figure 467. Cherry Tumbler, #7-9, 4.0" high, W (underlined) in Circle mark:
  Left: Purple Slag, 1977-84, $25-30.
  Middle: Caramel Slag, 1982, $25-30.
  Right: Ruby Slag, 1978, $25-30.

Figure 466. Cherry Goblet, #7-12, 6.4" high:
  Left: Purple Slag, 1977 & 1984, not marked & W (underlined) in Circle mark, $30-35.
  Right: Ruby Slag, c.1978, W (underlined) in Circle mark, $30-35.

Not shown: Cherry Goblet, #7-12, 6.4" high, Caramel Slag, 1982, W (underlined) in Circle mark, $30-35.

Figure 468.
  Left: Strawberry & Current Goblet, #77-36, 6.5" high, Purple Slag, date unknown, not marked, $40-45.
  Middle: Sawtooth Goblet, #77-35, 6.5" high, Purple Slag, 1966, not marked, $35-40.
  Right: Daisy & Cube Goblet, #77-21, 5.8" high, Purple Slag, c.1950, not marked, $65-75.

Figure 469. Lattice Open Edge Plate, mold number unknown, 10.0" wide, Purple Slag, c.1950, not marked, $65-75.

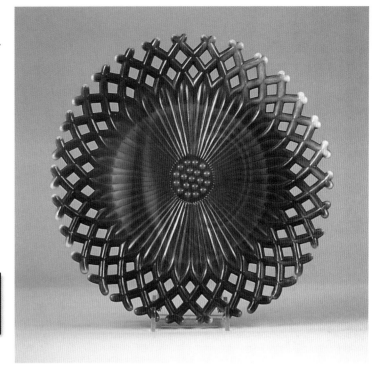

Not shown: Lattice Closed Edge Plate, mold number unknown, 10.3" wide, Purple Slag, c.1950, not marked, $65-75.

Figure 470. Horseshoe Ashtray, mold number unknown, 8.0" long, Purple Slag, date unknown, not marked, $40-45.

Figure 471. Daisy & Button Square Ashtray, #22-3, 5.7" wide, Purple Slag, 1966, not marked, $35-40.

Chapter 5

Fenton Art Glass Company

General History

Today, of all of the glass factories and companies mentioned in this book, the Fenton Art Glass Company is the most widely known. This is primarily because they are the largest, and one of very few American makers of decorative glass still in operation today. Blenko Glass in Milton, West Virginia, is one other surviving older company. To one degree or another, American manufacturers of pottery and glass have often competed with European and Asian made products. Today, glassware from China is abundant, and the pricing is very competitive. In many stores, it is difficult to find any pieces of American-made glassware. Despite this fact, and much to their credit, Fenton has maintained a place in the current giftware industry. Creative thinking, updated equipment and business practices, good leadership, the development of a strong collector base, and, of course, the production of beautiful glassware have been essential for survival. One recent, important sales and advertising approach was promoting and selling Fenton Glass on the QVC home shopping television channel.

Fenton is located in Williamstown, West Virginia, and has from the start been a family owned and operated business. Much like Blenko, their history is built on colored glass. At Fenton, color is everything. Unlike Blenko, their reputation of recent decades has been dominated by decorating those colors.

In 1905, Fenton started as a decorating company, but soon after, built their own factory. Unlike Imperial and Westmoreland, they produced relatively few utility and tabletop items. Instead, most of their output has focused on decorative pieces. Opalescent colors and Carnival Glass (they were the first to market it) was important in their early years. Many, many other colors followed as well as many treatments of glass, including coin dot, crimped edges, and crest items, where a thin band of a contrasting color is attached to the piece's outer edge. As with Imperial and Westmoreland, the popularity of Milk Glass, starting in the 1950s, was important to Fenton as well. Milk Glass in Fenton's Hobnail pattern became synonymous with their name. Also, the production of Cranberry pieces has been important for much of their history. A decorating department was reestablished in 1968, and has grown to be a very important aspect of their business. In the 1970s, Fenton also reintroduced Carnival Glass and developed several exotic colors such as Burmese, Rosalene, and Favrene. In recent years, their Connoisseur Collection has offered some of the most spectacular pieces of glass ever made in America.[13]

Figure 472. Example of "Fenton" script in oval mold mark. Also used is an "F" script in oval mark.

Slag History at Fenton and Private Productions

Fenton has used both the names Slag Glass and Marble Glass. As noted in Chapter 4, Fenton made a few pieces in Purple Slag for the L. G. Wright Glass Company in the 1950s. Fenton did not produce a Slag color for their catalog assortment until 1970 when Blue Marble was introduced. Unlike the boldness of Purple or Ruby Slag, Blue Marble was a soft blend of an opaque light blue mixed with Milk Glass. Most pieces were produced in either the Rose or Hobnail pattern. It was discontinued after four years; however, it must have sold well during that period considering how many pieces are consistently on the secondary market. These pieces can sometimes be found with the gold and black Fenton factory sticker used in that era, and a few pieces even have the removable section where the ware number and price were printed. Fenton has made other Slag items such as a few pieces for their 1994 spring supplement and small grouping sold exclusively in their gift shop. See Figures 489, 543 and 544. However, Blue Marble was the only Slag color offered for an extended period.

The other two colors that predominate in this chapter were both made by Fenton as private production collections for the Levay Distributing Company. See Chapter 3 for background information on Levay. The first was Purple Slag produced in 1981 (Fenton's color code is "PS"). Figure 473 shows a copy of the advertising flyer and the pieces in the assortment. Except for the Hobnail Bell, which is unmarked, all pieces carry a Fenton logo and "8" designating the 1980s. See Figure 472 for an example of a typical Fenton logo. With Fenton glass, if the full Fenton name is written in script in an oval, it means that the mold is original to the company. If the logo consists of a scripted "F" in an oval, the mold was acquired from another factory.

The second group made for Levay came in 1985 in Ruby Marble (Fenton's color code is "RX"). Figure 474 shows the advertising flyer for this assortment. From this group, only the epergne does not carry a Fenton mark and only some have the "8" designation for the 1980s.

Both the Purple Slag and the Ruby Marble can be found with Fenton's gold and black stickers. Fenton's mold numbers were used for all of these private production items for Levay. Aside from these Slag items, Fenton made many other beautiful collections for Levay in colors including Aqua Opal Carnival, Burmese, Chocolate, Deep Plum Opalescent, and Red Sunset Carnival.[14]

Over the years, we have found many non-catalog Slag items by Fenton made for a variety of reasons. Some were private productions for club or special event promotions, some were produced for Fenton's gift shop, and some were undoubtedly produced as samples. Whatever the reason, finding an odd piece of Slag by Fenton is not unusual. Of course, this is great for collectors, like ourselves, who love Slag Glass! We have included examples of some of these in the photographs even though they were produced in years beyond the titled years of this book.

A Limited Offering for the Antique Trade

PURPLE SLAG

The spellbinding beauty of Fenton's timeless "Purple Slag" collection is sure to please all collectors of fine American made glassware. Through the years, beginning with the first production of variegated colored glass around 1850 "Slag Glass" has had, and will always have, a magical appeal. The luscious shading and inter mixing of vibrant colors has had several names over the years, including Marble Glass and End of Day Glass, depending on the manufacturer. No two pieces of Slag Glass are alike, each reflecting the individuality of the glass craftsman and the inherent individuality of the glass itself. From the kitten slipper to the grape and cable tobacco jar the ageless artistry is recreated for the collectors of generations to come.

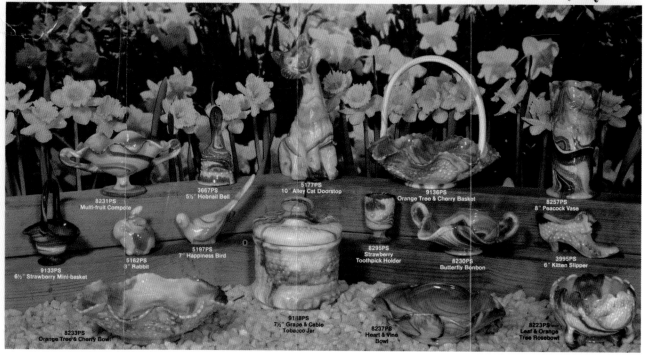

Figure 473. Copy of the advertising flyer from the Levay Distributing Company in conjunction with Fenton showing 15 pieces available in Purple Slag, 1981.

A Limited Offering for the Antique Trade

RUBY MARBLE

The spellbinding beauty of Fenton's timeless "Ruby Marble" collection is sure to please all collectors of fine American made glassware. Through the years, beginning with the first production of variegated colored glass around 1850 "Marble Glass" has had, and will always have, a magical appeal. The luscious shading and inter mixing of vibrant colors has had several names over the years, including Slag Glass and End of Day Glass, depending on the manufacturer. No two pieces of Marble Glass are alike, each reflecting the individuality of the glass craftsman and the inherent individuality of the glass itself. From the hen on a nest to the grape and cable tobacco jar the ageless artistry is recreated for the collectors of generations to come.

Figure 474. Copy of the advertising flyer from the Levay Distributing Company in conjunction with Fenton showing 14 pieces available in Ruby Marble, 1985.

Figure 475.
  Left: Sitting Bear, #5151, 3.6" high, Ruby Marble, private production (non-catalog) for Levay Distributing Co., 1985, Fenton script in oval mark, $95+.
  Right: Duckling, #5169, 3.2" high, Purple Marble (non-catalog), c.1981, Fenton script in oval mark, $125+.

Figure 476. Bunny (Rabbit), #5162, 3.2" high, Fenton script in oval mark:
  Left: Ruby Marble, private production (non-catalog) for Levay Distributing Co., 1985, $85+.
  Right: Purple Slag, private production (non-catalog) for Levay Distributing Co., 1981, $100+.

Figure 477.
  Left: Fawn on bust-off (non-catalog), #5160, 6.3" high, Ruby Marble, 1985, Fenton script in oval mark, $150+.
  Right: Fawn, #5160, 3.5" high, Ruby Marble, private production (non-catalog) for Levay Distributing Co., 1985, Fenton script in oval mark, $75+.

Figure 478. Happiness Bird, #5197, 6.8" long, Purple Slag, private production (non-catalog) for Levay Distributing Co., 1981, Fenton script in oval mark, $75+.

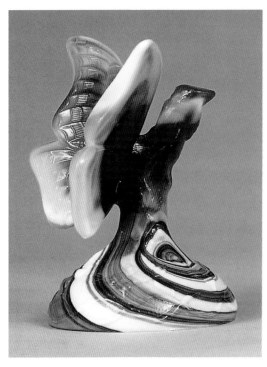

Figure 479. Butterfly on Branch, #5171, 4.9" high, Ruby Marble, private production (non-catalog) for Levay Distributing Co., 1985, Fenton script in oval mark, $75+.

Figure 480.
Left: Donkey, #5125, 4.5" long, Ruby Marble (non-catalog), date unknown, not marked, $75+.
Right: Clown, #5205, 4.0" high, Ruby Marble Carnival (non-catalog), c.1990, Fenton script in oval mark, $75+.

Figure 481. Blown Egg, 2.2" high, Blue Marble (non-catalog), 1970s, not marked, $65+.

Figure 482. Alley Cat Doorstop, #5177, 10.8" high, Purple Slag, private production (non-catalog) for Levay Distributing Co., 1981, Fenton script in oval mark, $600+.

Figure 484. Fox Covered Dish, mold number unknown, 7.1" long, Ruby Marble (non-catalog), c.1993, F in oval mark, $350+. Westmoreland previously owned this mold.

Figure 485. Hen Covered Dish, #5186, 5.4" long, Fenton script in oval mark:
   Left: Ruby Marble, private production (non-catalog) for Levay Distributing Co., 1985, $95+.
   Right: Blue Marble, 1971-72, $40-45.

Figure 483. Alley Cat Doorstop, #5177, 10.8" high, Ruby Marble, private production (non-catalog) for Levay Distributing Co., 1985, Fenton script in oval mark, $750+.

Figure 486. Large Hen Covered Dish (Smooth Rim base), #5182, 8.0" long, Purple Marble (non-catalog), date unknown, not marked, $250+.

Figure 488. Large Rooster Covered Dish, #4680, 7.1" long, Ruby Marble (non-catalog), c.1993, F in oval mark, $350+. Westmoreland previously owned this mold.

Figure 487. Large Hen Covered Dish (Scalloped base), #5182, 8.3" long, Blue Marble, 1971-72, Fenton script in oval mark, $85-95.

Figure 489. Two examples of Plum Slag, 1994:
  Left: Large Rooster Covered Dish, #4680, 7.1" long, F in oval mark, $85-100. Westmoreland previously owned this mold.
  Right: Hen Covered Dish, #5186, 5.4" long, Fenton script in oval mark, $50-60.

Figure 490. Ashtray & Pipe Holder, mold number unknown, 5.6" wide, Green Marble (non-catalog?), date unknown, not marked, $45+.

Figure 491. Rose Ashtray, #9271, 7.2" wide, Blue Marble, 1970-71, not marked, $30-35.

Figure 492. Hobnail 3-Piece Ashtray Set, #3610, small 3.5" wide, medium 5.0" wide, large 6.5" wide, Blue Marble, 1970-72, not marked, $95-110 set.

Figure 493.
   Left: Hobnail Bell, #983, 5.6" high, Purple production (non-catalog) for Levay Distributing Co., 1981, not
   marked, $75+.
   Right: Strawberry Toothpick Holder, #8295, 3.0" high, Purple
   Slag, private production (non-catalog) for Levay Distributing Co., 1981, Fenton script in oval mark, $35+.

Figure 495. Small Regency Basket, #8634, 7.0" high, Ruby
Marble, private production (non-catalog) for Levay Distributing
Co., 1985, F in oval mark, $100+.

Figure 494. Strawberry Mini-Basket, #9133, 5.5" high, Purple
Slag, private production (non-catalog) for Levay Distributing
Co., 1981, Fenton script in oval mark, $75+.

Figure 496. Hobnail Basket, double crimped, #3736, 7.2" high,
Blue Marble, 1970-73, not marked, $40-45.

Figure 497. Large Regency Basket, #8635, 9.6" wide, Ruby Marble, private production (non-catalog) for Levay Distributing Co., 1985, F in oval mark, $225+.

Figure 499. Orange Tree & Cherry Basket, crimped, #9136, 10.0" wide, Purple Slag, private production (non-catalog) for Levay Distributing Co., 1981, Fenton script in oval mark, $225+.

Figure 498. Rose Crimped Basket, double crimped, #9235, 9.0" wide, Blue Marble, 1970-73, not marked, $75-85.

Figure 500. Small Basket, crimped, mold number unknown, 4.4" high, Ruby Marble Carnival (non-catalog), 1996, Fenton script in oval mark, $50+.

Figure 503. Butterfly 2-Handled Bonbon, crimped, #8230, 8.6"
long, Purple Slag, private production (non-catalog) for Levay
Distributing Co., 1981, Fenton script in oval mark, $85+.

Figure 501. Orange Tree & Cherry Bowl, crimped, #8233, 10.0"
wide, Purple Slag, private production (non-catalog) for Levay
Distributing Co., 1981, Fenton script in oval mark, $125+.

Figure 504. Leaf & Orange Tree Rosebowl, #8223, 5.5" wide,
Purple Slag, private production (non-catalog) for Levay Distributing Co., 1981, Fenton script in oval mark, $95+.

Figure 502. Heart & Vine Bowl, crimped, #8237, 8.6" wide, Purple
Slag, private production (non-catalog) for Levay Distributing Co.,
1981, Fenton script in oval mark, $95+.

Figure 505. Grape & Cable Bowl, double crimped, #9027, 9.0" wide, Ruby Marble, private production (non-catalog) for Levay Distributing Co., 1985, Fenton script in oval mark, $225+.

Figure 506. Grape & Cable Cuspidor, #9058, 6.8" wide, Ruby Marble, private production (non-catalog) for Levay Distributing Co., 1985, Fenton script in oval mark, $225+.

Figure 507. Regency Cupped Bowl, #8623, 6.3" wide, Ruby Marble, private production (non-catalog) for Levay Distributing Co., 1985, script F mark, $125+.

Figure 508. Rose Bowl, #9224, 7.0" wide, Blue Marble, 1970-73, not marked, $40-45.

Figure 511.
   Left: Hobnail Bonbon with metal handle, crimped, #3706, 7.7" wide, Blue Marble, 1970-73, not marked, $30-35.
   Right: Hobnail Bonbon, crimped, #3706, 7.6" wide, Blue Marble (non-catalog), 1970s, not marked, $30+.

Figure 509. Rose Bowl, double crimped, #9225, 9.2" wide, Blue Marble, 1970-73, not marked, $50-55.

Figure 510. Hobnail Heart Dish, crimped, #3733, 7.4" long, Blue Marble, 1970-72, not marked, $55-60.

Figure 512.
   Left: Hobnail Compote, crimped, #3628, 6.0" high, Blue Marble, 1970-73, not marked, $25-30.
   Right: Rose Compote, crimped, #9223, 6.4" high, Blue Marble, 1970-73, not marked, $25-30.

Figure 514. Hobnail Compote (Footed Bowl), crimped, #3731, 9.5" wide, Blue Marble, 1970-73, not marked, $45-50.

Figure 513. Multi-fruit Compote, crimped, #8231, 8.6" wide, Purple Slag, private production (non-catalog) for Levay Distributing Co., 1981, Fenton script in oval mark, $95+.

Figure 515. Hobnail Compote, flared square, mold number unknown, 6.0" high, Ruby Marble (non-catalog), date unknown, $175+.

Figure 518. Rose Footed Covered Dish, #9284, 8.3" high, Blue Marble, 1970-73, not marked, $40-45.

Figure 516. Rose Compote, #9222, 7.5" high, Blue Marble, 1970-73, not marked or Fenton script in oval mark, $35-40.v

Figure 519. Hobnail Covered Footed Dish, #3886, 6.5" wide, Blue Marble, 1970-73, not marked, $40-45.

Figure 517. The Rose Compote (#9222) had two designs in the bowl:
  Left: Smooth surface, Fenton script in oval mark.
  Right: Ribbed surface, not marked.

Figure 520. Grape & Cable Tobacco (Cookie) Covered Jar, #9188, 7.4" high, Purple Slag, private production (non-catalog) for Levay Distributing Co., 1981, Fenton script in oval mark, $400+.

Figure 522. Grape & Cable Tobacco (Cookie) Covered Jar, #9188, 7.4" high, Blue Marble, 1971, not marked, $175-200.

Figure 521. Grape & Cable Tobacco (Cookie) Covered Jar, #9188, 7.4" high, Ruby Marble, private production (non-catalog) for Levay Distributing Co., 1985, Fenton script in oval mark, $400+.

Figure 523. Regency Covered Butter Dish, #8680, 7.2" wide, Ruby Marble, private production (non-catalog) for Levay Distributing Co., 1985, F in oval mark, $200+.

Figure 524. Flute (Colonial) Pattern Butter Dish, mold number unknown, 7.4" wide, Ruby Marble (non-catalog), 1990s, script F mark, $300+. Westmoreland previously owned this mold.

Figure 526. Lace Edge Dog Face Plate, mold number unknown, 6" wide, Ruby Marble (non-catalog), c.1991, not marked, $75+. Westmoreland previously owned this mold.

Figure 525.
   Left: Christmas in America, Plate #4 (St. Mary's in the Mountains), #8270, 8.0" wide, Purple Marble (non-catalog), 1973, Fenton script in oval mark, $150+.
   Right: Christmas in America, Plate #1 (Little Brown Church in the Vale), #8270, 8.0" wide, Blue Marble, satin finish, 1970, Fenton script in oval mark, $65-75.

Figure 527.
  Left: Rose Candleholder, #9270, 3.5" high, Blue
    Marble, 1970-72, not marked, $40-45 pair.
  Right: Hobnail Candleholder, #3974, 3.5" high, Blue
    Marble, 1970-72, not marked, $40-45 pair.

Figure 528. Hobnail Candle Bowl (holds six candles), #3872, 6.5" wide, Blue Marble, 1970-73, not marked, $25-30 each.

Figure 530.
  Left: Hobnail Votive Candleholder, #3647, 3.9" high, Ruby
    Marble (non-catalog), 1990s, Fenton script in oval mark,
    $75+.
  Right: Dish whimsey (non-catalog) from Hobnail Votive Can-
    dleholder (#3647), 4.1" wide, Ruby Marble, 1990s, Fenton
    script in oval mark, $75+.

Figure 529. Colonial Candleholder, #9071, 8.5" high, Ruby
Marble (non-catalog), 1990s,
not marked, $125+ each.

Figure 531.
  Left: Butterfly Mug, mold number unknown, 3.1" high, Ruby
    Marble, private production (non-catalog) for Fenton Art
    Glass Collectors of America, 1987, FAGCA mark, $50+.
  Middle: Cup whimsey (non-catalog) from Butterfly Mug, 3.7"
    high, Ruby Marble, 1987, FAGCA mark, $75+.
  Right: Dish whimsey (non-catalog) from Butterfly Mug,
    crimped, 5.0" wide, Ruby Marble, 1987, FAGCA mark,
    $85+.

Figure 534. Hobnail Covered Slipper, #3700, 6.3" long, Blue Marble, 1971-73, not marked, $45-50.

Figure 532. Daisy & Button Cat Shoe, #1995, 5.9" long, Ruby Marble (non-catalog), date unknown, Fenton script in oval mark, $65+.

Figure 535. Daisy & Button Bootie, #1994, 4.2" long, Purple Slag, private production (non-catalog) for L. G. Wright, c.1953, not marked, $45+.

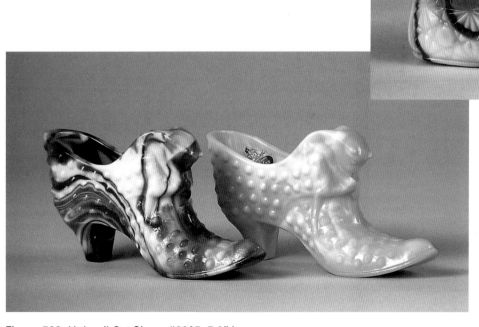

Figure 533. Hobnail Cat Shoe, #3995, 5.9" long:
    Left: Purple Slag, private production (non-catalog) for Levay Distributing Co., 1981,
        Fenton script in oval mark, $65+.
    Right: Blue Marble, 1970-73, not marked, $20-25.

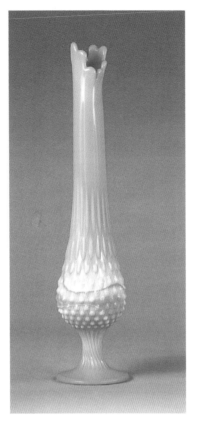

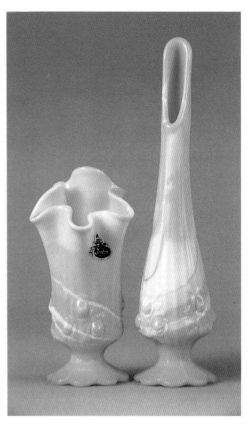

Figure 536. Peacock Vase, #8257, 7.8" high, Purple Slag, private production (non-catalog) for Levay Distributing Co., 1981, Fenton script in oval mark, $150+.

Figure 537. Hobnail Footed Swung Vase, #3753, 14-16" high, Blue Marble, 1970-72, not marked, $35-40.

Figure 538.
  Left: Rose Swung Handkerchief Vase, #9254, 5-7" high, Blue Marble, 1970-73, not marked, $25-30.
  Right: Rose Swung Bud Vase, #9256, 9-11" high, Blue Marble, 1970-73, not marked, $25-30.

Figure 539. Thumbprint 4-Piece Epergne, crimped, #4401, 9.0" high, Ruby Marble, private production (non-catalog) for Levay Distributing Co., 1985, not marked, $475+.

Figure 540. Ribbed Fan Vase, #847, 4.8" high, Purple Marble (non-catalog), 1980s, Fenton script in oval mark, $175+.

Figure 542. Hobnail Snowcrest Vase, crimped, mold number unknown, 5.8" high, Purple Marble (non-catalog), c.2002, Fenton script in oval mark, $95+.

Figure 541. Wheat Silvercrest Vase, crimped, #5858, 8" high, Purple Marble (non-catalog), 1980s, not marked, $225+.

Figure 543. Two examples of Sea Mist Slag, 1994:
Left: Duckling, #5212, 2.5" long, not marked, $35-40.
Right: Atlantis Vase, #5150, 6.5" high, for Fenton Gift Shop
(non-catalog), Fenton script in oval mark, $125+.

Figure 544. Five examples of "Almost Heaven" (named by Bill Fenton) Blue Slag, 1989 for Fenton Gift
Shop (non-catalog), left to right:
Butterfly on Branch, #5171, 4.9" high, Fenton script in oval mark, $75+.
Drapery Cat Shoe, #5290, 6.0" long, satin finish, Fenton script in oval mark, $35+.
Hobnail Basket, double crimped, #3736, 7.2" high, not marked, $95+.
Hobnail Bonbon with metal handle, crimped, #3706, 7.9" wide, not marked, $65+.
Hobnail Candleholder, #3674, 5.7" high, Fenton script in oval mark, $150+ pair.

Chapter 6

Slag Glass from Other Companies

A number of other companies have made Slag Glass since Victorian times, including some that are operating today. We thought it was important to provide at least a sampling of some of these items and companies that have made or sold Slag. Included are photographs with examples from the following companies:

George Davidson & Company, England, 1867-1987.

L. J. Houze Convex Glass Company, Point Marion, Pennsylvania, 1902-present.

Akro Agate Company, Clarksburg, West Virginia, 1911-1951.

Degenhart's Crystal Art Glass Company, Cambridge, Ohio, 1947-1978.

Boyd's Crystal Art Glass, Cambridge, Ohio, 1978-present.

Guernsey Glass Company, (Harold & Judy Bennett), Cambridge, Ohio, 1967-1990s.

John K. Kemple Glass Works, East Palestine, Ohio, 1945-1970.

Kanawha Glass Company, Dunbar, West Virginia, 1955-1987.

L. E. Smith Glass Company, Mount Pleasant, Pennsylvania, 1907-present.

Plum Glass Company, Pittsburgh, Pennsylvania, 1984-present.

Rosso Wholesale Glass, Port Vue, Pennsylvania, 1980-present.

Summit Art Glass Company, Revenna, Ohio, 1972-2005.

Mosser Glass, Cambridge, Ohio, 1971-present.

The overall quality of American-made Slag Glass is very good. Collectors will sometimes be dogmatic in their views that the quality of glass from one company is superior to another. We do not generally hold that view. Small factories may have more difficulties with quality control, but large factories also have their share of problems.

Several import companies have had Slag Glass made in Taiwan. As already mentioned in Chapter 3, some Westmoreland molds have been reproduced or copied. The Three Kittens 7" Plate (#KP-1) and Chick on Oval Two-handled Basket (#CK-1) are two that have been made in Purple Slag and have the WG mold mark. The Oval Duck Covered Dish (#OD-1) and the Standing Rooster Covered Dish (#SR-1) are two molds that have been copied. See Figures 279 and 295 for comparison between the Westmoreland and Import molds. Another Westmoreland mold that has not yet appeared in a Slag color but has also been copied is the Eagle Covered Dish (#EA-1). Several L. G. Wright molds were purchased when that factory closed and are being used including the Pump and Tough (#77-95 & #77-96) although we have not yet seen these in Slag. Besides what are shown in these photographs, Slag items from Taiwan can be found in many other molds including butter dishes, hand ring holders, rolling pins, salt and pepper sets, reamers, and egg trays. In the past, the quality of the import pieces has been rather poor, but we have seen recent samples proving that the quality is getting considerably better.

Figure 545. Cloud Glass by George Davidson, English, 1920-30s.

Figure 546. Slag Glass lamp from L. J. Houze Convex Glass Co., 1920s.

Figure 548. Slag Vase from unknown maker. These can be found in several Slag colors, c.1913.

Figure 547. Slag Glass items from the Akro Agate Co., 1930-40s.

Figure 549. Slag Glass items from Degenhart's Crystal Art Glass Co., 1960s -1978.

Figure 550. Slag Glass items from Boyd's Crystal Art Glass, 1978-present.

Figure 551. Slag Glass items from Guernsey Glass Co., 1970-90s.

Figure 552. Three Rocky Horses from Guernsey Glass Co., 1981-82, part of a 12 color series. The Caramel Slag (their color name was Buster Brown, #7) & Purple Slag (Arabian Nights, #12) were made by Mosser for Guernsey and the Ruby Slag (Carousel Slag, #1) was made by Westmoreland.

Figure 554. Slag Glass (their name was End-of-Day) 5" Cat Covered Dish from John K. Kemple Glassworks, 1960s.

Figure 553. Slag Glass (their name was End-of-Day) items from John K. Kemple Glassworks, 1960s.

Figure 555. Slag Glass (their name was End of Day) items from Kanawha Glass Co., 1970s.

Figure 556. Red Slag Glass (End of Day) Large Hen Covered Dish, satin finish, from Kanawha Glass Co. 1970s.

Figure 557. Blue Slag Glass items from Avon Products, 1978.

Figure 558. Doric Blue Slag candleholder from Plum Glass Co., 1990s, not marked. Westmoreland previously owned this mold.

Figure 559. Examples from Mosser Glass, 1971-present.. Left to Right: Two Jenny Dolls made for Vi Hunter Glass as part of a series, 1979-82; Love Birds Covered Dish, previously Westmoreland mold, Purple Slag, not marked; Large Hen Covered Dish, previously L. G. Wright mold, Red Slag, M in Ohio Outline mark; Hen Covered Dish, Blue & Red Slag, not marked; Small Hen Covered Dish, previously L. G. Wright mold, Red Slag, not marked.

Figure 560. Almond Nouveau items from L. E. Smith Glass Co., 1980-82.

Figure 561. Chocolate Slag bowl from L. E. Smith Glass Co., c.1980. This is a true Chocolate Slag in that orange and brown are mixed with a Chocolate Glass base color.

Figure 562. Examples from Rosso Wholesale Glass, 1990s-present, previously Westmoreland molds. Left to Right: Mule Eared Rabbit Covered Dish, Purple & White Slag Carnival, Westmoreland Circle mark & WG mark; Hen Covered Dish, Purple & White Slag, Westmoreland Circle mark; Owl on Books, Blue & White Slag, WG mark; Owl on Books, Green & White Slag, WG mark; Standing Rooster Covered Dish, Green & White Slag, R in Keystone mark (mold can also be found unmarked); Rooster Covered Dish, Red & White Slag, Westmoreland Circle mark.

Figure 563. Examples from Rosso Wholesale Glass, 1990s-present. Left to Right: Small Hen Covered Dish, previously Westmoreland mold, Purple & White Slag, R in Keystone mark on top & WG mark on bottom; Bull Covered Dish, previously L. G. Wright mold, Purple & White Slag, R in Keystone mark; Beehive Covered Dish, previously L. G. Wright mold, Caramel & White Slag, not marked; Hen Covered Dish, previously Westmoreland mold, Blue & White Slag, Westmoreland Circle mark; Cat Covered Dish, previously Westmoreland mold, Red & White Slag, Westmoreland Circle mark.

Figure 564. Purple Slag Glass from Mirror Images, 2002-03, previously Imperial molds. Left to Right: Imperial Sign, Purple Slag Carnival, MI mark; Imperial Sign, Purple Slag, MI mark; Venus Rising (Bashful Charlotte), Purple Slag, IG & 81 mark; Candlewick Covered Dish, Purple Slag, not marked.

Figure 565. Examples from Summit Art Glass Co., 1972-2005, previously Westmoreland molds. Left to Right: Chick on Egg Pile Covered Dish, Carmel, 1992, WG mark; Oval Duck Covered Dish, Patriot Slag, 1997, Westmoreland Circle mark; Oval Duck Covered Dish, Carmel, 1992, Westmoreland Circle mark. For later colors of the Oval Duck Covered Dish, Summit changed the Westmoreland Circle mark to a WG mark. Some Carmel items are a lighter color.

Figure 566. Examples from Summit Art Glass Co., 1972-2005, previously Westmoreland molds. Left to Right: Camel Covered Dish, Purple Slag, 1996, Westmoreland Circle mark; Santa on Sleigh Covered Dish, Red Slag Carnival, 2001, WG mark; Camel Covered Dish, Geraldine Delight Red, 1996, Westmoreland Circle mark.

Figure 567. Examples from Summit Art Glass Co., 1972-2005, previously Westmoreland molds. Left to Right: Rooster Covered Dish, Blue & Orange Slag, 1994, Westmoreland Circle mark; Clock, Purple Slag, 1996, not marked; Chick on 2-Handled Basket, Red Slag, c.1994, WG mark & V in Circle mark; Duck Salt Dip, Amber & Grey Slag, c.1994, WG mark.

Figure 568. Examples of Owl Covered Jars from Summit Art Glass Co., 1972-2005, previously Imperial mold, all have ALIG mark. (Note – all original Imperial Slag Owl Jars have an IG mark.) Left to Right: Carmel, 1992; Purple Slag Carnival, 1996, Red & White Slag Carnival, 2001, Geraldine Delight Red, 1996, Malachite Green Slag, 1998.

Figure 569. Examples from Summit Art Glass Co., 1972-2005, previously Imperial molds. Left to Right: Owl Cream & Sugar Set, Purple Slag, 1996, IG & faint V in Circle mark; Owl Covered Jar, Purple Slag, 1996, ALIG mark; Owl Sugar, Blue Slag, c.2004, McK mark.

Figure 570. Examples from Summit Art Glass Co., 1972-2005, previously Westmoreland molds. Left to Right: Large Hen Covered Dish, Purple Slag, 1996, WG mark; Turtle Covered Dish, Purple Slag, 1996, not marked; Chick on Egg Pile Covered Dish, Purple Slag, 1996, WG mark.

Figure 571. Imported Purple Slag items from Taiwan, 1980s to present.

Figure 572. Imported Purple Slag items from Taiwan, 1980s to present. Westmoreland previously owned the Three Kittens Plate mold in upper right corner, WG mark.

Figure 573. After a careful comparison, we found that this "JUST A THIMBLE FULL" Toothpick Holder was copied from an English version (c.1880s) by Davidson; however we have been unable to determine its US maker.

Endnotes

[1]Patricia McCulley, "English Purple Slag Glass." *Glass Collector's Digest*, December/January 2000, Vol. XIII, No. 4, pp. 83-87.

[2]William Heacock, "Slag Glass From Around The World." *Collecting Glass: Research, Reprints & Reviews* (Richardson Printing Corp., Marietta, Ohio, 1984), pp.39-54.

[3]McCulley, p. 83.

[4]Ruth Webb Lee, *Early American Pressed Glass* (Charles E. Tuttle Co., Inc., Rutland, Vermont, 1985), p. 619. Originally published by the author, Pittsford, NY, 1931.

[5]James Measell, ed. *Imperial Glass Encyclopedia*, Volume 1 (Antique Publications, Marietta, Ohio, 1995), pp. viii-xxv.

[6]Ron Doll, "Lucile Remembers," *The Imperial Collectors Glasszette*, April 1994, Vol. 17, Issue 4, p.9.

[7]Kathy Doub, "The National Treasures Collection by Sears, Roebuck and Co." *The Imperial Collectors Glasszette*, October 2000, Vol. 24, Issue 2, pp. 4-5.

[8]Lorraine Kovar, *Westmoreland Glass 1950-1984* (Antique Publications, Marietta, Ohio, 1991), pp. 8-10.

[9]Tom Felt and Elaine & Rich Stoer, *The Glass Candlestick Book, Volume 3* (Collector Books, Paducah, Kentucky, 2005), pp. 269-270.

[10]Kovar, pp. 11-12.

[11]James Measell and W. C. "Red" Roetteis, *The L. G. Wright Glass Company* (Antique Publications, Marietta, Ohio, 1997), pp. 8-50.

[12]Doll, p.9.

[13]Alan Linn, *The Fenton Story of Glass Making*, Revised Edition (Fenton Art Glass Co. publication, Williamstown, West Virginia, 1995), pp. 1-13.

[14]Carrie and Gerald Domitz, *Fenton, Glass Made for Other Companies* (Collector Books, Paducah, Kentucky, 2005), pp. 69-77.

In writing this book, we referred numerous times to the set *The Glass Candlestick Book, Volumes 1, 2, and 3* by Tom Felt, Elaine & Rich Stoer. They have proved to be an excellent source for checking facts and providing a general background on American glass factories.

Bibliography

Archer, Margaret & Douglas. *Imperial Glass*. Paducah, KY: Collector Books, 1978.

Belknap, E. M. *Milk Glass*. New York: Crown Publishers, 1959.

Bennett, Judy. Personal Interview. July 10, 2006.

Boyd's Crystal Art Glass. *Boyd's Crystal Art Glass*. Cambridge, OH: Boyd's Crystal Art Glass, 1990.

Bredehoft, Neila & Tom. *Heisey Glass: 1896-1957, Identification and Value Guide*. Paducah, KY: Collector Books, 2001.

Burkholder, John R. and D. Thomas O'Conner. *Kemple Glass: 1945-1970*. Marietta, OH: Antique Publications, 1997.

Burns, Carl O. *Imperial Carnival Glass: Identification and Value Guide*. Paducah, KY: Collector Books, 1996.

Coe, Debbie & Randy. *Glass Animals & Figurines*. Atglen, PA: Schiffer Publishing Ltd., 2003.

"Davidson English Pressed Glass," *Online Glass Museum: New Zealand*. May 20, 2006, http://www.glass.co.nz/Davidson.htm.

Doll, Ron. "Lucile Remembers," *The Imperial Collectors Glasszette*, April 1994, pp.9-10.

Domitz, Carrie & Gerald. *Fenton Glass Made for Other Companies*. Paducah, KY: Collector Books, 2005.

Doub, Kathy. "The National Treasures Collection by Sears, Roebuck and Company" *The Imperial Collectors Glasszette*, October 2000, pp. 4-5.

Felt, Tom, Elaine & Rich Stoer. *The Glass Candlestick Book, Volume 1*. Paducah, KY: Collector Books, 2003.

-----. *The Glass Candlestick Book, Volume 2*. Paducah, KY: Collector Books, 2003.

-----. *The Glass Candlestick Book, Volume 3*. Paducah, KY: Collector Books, 2005.

Fenton Art Glass Co. catalogs & price lists, 1970-1973, 1994.

Garrison, Myrna & Bob. *Milk Glass: Imperial Glass Corporation*. Atglen, PA: Schiffer Publishing Ltd., 2001.

Grizel, Ruth. *American Slag Glass*. Paducah, KY: Collector Books, 1998.

Hahn, Frank L., & Paul Kikeli. *Heisey and Heisey by Imperial Glass Animals*. Lima, OH: Golden Era Publications, 1991.

Heacock, William. "Slag Glass From Around the World," *Collecting Glass: Research, Reprints and Reviews, Volume 1*. Marietta, OH: Antique Publications, 1984.

-----. *Fenton Glass: The First Twenty-five Years*. Marietta, OH: O-Val Advertising Corp., 1979.

-----. *Fenton Glass: The Second Twenty-five Years*. Marietta, OH: O-Val Advertising Corp., 1980.

-----. *Fenton Glass: The Third Twenty-five Years*. Marietta, OH: O-Val Advertising Corp., 1989.

Heacock, William, James Measell & Berry Wiggins. *Harry Northwood: The Early Years 1881-1900*. Marietta, OH: Antique Publications, 1990.

Imperial catalogs & price lists, 1959-1983.

Kennedy, Lucile. Personal Interview, July 27, 2006.

Kovar, Lorraine. *Westmoreland Glass, 1950-1984*. Marietta, OH: Antique Publications, 1991.

-----. *Westmoreland Glass, 1950-1984: Volume II*. Marietta, OH: Antique Publications, 1991.

-----. *Westmoreland Glass: Volume III, 1888-1940*. Marietta, OH: Antique Publications, 1997.

-----. *Westmoreland Glass: The Popular Years, 1940-1985*. Paducah, KY: Collector Books, 2004.

Lee, Ruth Webb. *Early American Pressed Glass*, *Enlarged and Revised*. Rutland, Vermont: Charles E. Tuttle Co., Inc., 1985. Originally published by the author, Pittsford, NY, 1931.

-----. *Victorian Glass*. Rutland, Vermont: Charles E. Tuttle Co., Inc., 1985. Originally published by the author, Pittsford, NY, 1944.

Levay Distributing Co. advertising flyers & price lists, 1977-1985.

Levi, Dodie & Gary. Personal Interview, August 10, 2005.

Levi, Gary. Personal Interview, July 12, 2006.

Linn, Alan. *The Fenton Story of Glass Making, Revised Edition*. Williamstown, WV: Fenton Art Glass Co., 1995.

Longwell, Kent P. Personal Interview. June 1, 2006.

Marsh, Laura J. *Imperial Glass: Lace Edge*. Atglen, PA: Schiffer Publishing Ltd., 2004.

McCulley, Patricia. "English Purple Slag Glass," *Glass Collector's Digest*, December/January 2000, pp. 83-87.

Measell, James, editor. *Fenton Glass: The 1980s Decade*. Marietta, OH: Antique Publications, 1996.

-----. *Fenton Glass: The 1990s Decade*. Marietta, OH: Antique Publications, 2000.

-----. *Imperial Glass Encyclopedia: Volume I*. Marietta, OH: Antique Publications, 1995.

-----. *Imperial Glass Encyclopedia: Volume II*. Marietta, OH: Antique Publications, 1997.

-----. *Imperial Glass Encyclopedia: Volume III*. Marietta, OH: Antique Publications, 1999.

Measell, James, & W. C. "Red" Roetteis. *The L. G. Wright Glass Company*. Marietta, OH: Antique Publications, 1997.

National Cambridge Collectors, Incorporated *Colors In Cambridge Glass*. Paducah, KY: Collector Books, 1984.

Newbound, Betty & Bill. *Collector's Encyclopedia of Milk Glass*. Paducah, KY: Collector Books, 1995.

Oard, Paul, & Lee Wilkerson. "Levay Glass," *Glass Collector's Digest*, February 1981, pp. 56-58.

Rosso, Phil, Jr., Personal Interview. July 14, 2006.

Shaeffer, Barbara. "Summit Art," *Glass Collector's Digest*, February 1985, pp. 24-31.

Wakefield, Hugh. *Nineteenth Century British Glass*. London: Faber and Faber Limited, 1982.

West Virginia Museum of American Glass, Ltd. *L. G. Wright Glass*. Atglen, PA: Schiffer Publishing Ltd., 2003.

Westmoreland catalogs & price lists, 1972-1982.

Wilson, Chas West. *Westmoreland Glass*. Paducah, KY: Collector Books, 1996.

Wright (L. G.) catalogs & price lists, 1960s-1990s.

Index